D0860270

American Literature

Cesare Pavese
AMERICAN LITERATURE
Essays and Opinions

TRANSLATED BY EDWIN FUSSELL

UNIVERSITY OF CALIFORNIA PRESS
BERKELEY LOS ANGELES
LONDON 1970

University of California Press
Berkeley and Los Angeles, California

University of California Press, Ltd.
London, England

SBN 520-01633-5
Library of Congress Catalog Card Number: 70-101338

Designed by Douglas Nicholson
Printed in the United States of America

Foreword

La politica è l'arte del possibile. Tutta la vita è politica (15 May 1939)

Cesare Pavese is one of those exotic names which for several decades have drifted along the edges of the American literary and intellectual consciousness. It is fairly well known in this country that Pavese was a poet of considerable promise, and a novelist of consummate if narrow power. In certain circles, it is also known that Pavese was a trenchant and widely ranging literary critic, and a prodigious translator, chiefly from the American. Surely he was the leading Italian Americanist—virtually a profession in Italy—of his generation, which came to maturity, was tormented, even slaughtered, yet somehow survived to transcend and transform the age of Mussolini. Pavese's novels have fared best in this country, and are now in the process of genuine translation by R. W. Flint. *Dialogues With Leucò,* Pavese's demythologized retelling of ancient myths, has been handsomely translated by William Arrowsmith and D. S. Carne-Ross. The poetry must obviously await a translator of rare and sympathetic talent. The literary criticism, especially the abundant work on American literature, can be more easily supplied than any of these, and indeed its appearance in English, considering how much of it is concerned with works in

English, is disgracefully overdue. The general drift of this criticism and some of its implications have been hinted by a number of American scholars, and several isolated excerpts have been more or less rendered. That Pavese has still made so little impact on American consciousness of American literature is owing to two obvious facts: first, that no description of criticism can replace the criticism itself; second, that no brief selections can carry any live sense of his quality. He was preeminently the kind of critic who has to be read in the large or not at all.

Like D. H. Lawrence, the other great foreign writer who was also a distinguished critic of American literature, Pavese was a nonacademic critic, though he was far less anti-academic (or anti-intellectual) than Lawrence. Naturally, there was a good deal about American writing he never knew, though a generous reader is likely to be impressed by how much he found out. There are, of course, a number of issues on which he disagreed with standard American criticism, for example, the overemphasis on "Puritanism," the insistence on the Poe-like construction of *Moby-Dick,* the absolute centrality of Sherwood Anderson for modern fiction. Such disagreements should be welcomed, for it is precisely when Pavese, with all that wild, original energy of discovery of his (which had, in the first instance, the purpose of using American literature to subvert Italian literature, thought, sensibility, and culture), departs from standard American criticism that the work of international understanding most tellingly commences, not now for him but for us. What was there in Pavese, in his culture, in his situation, that made him sometimes see us so differently than we see ourselves, as seen by our own critics? And what, to speak closer to home, can we still learn from his conservative humanism or from his radical anti-Fascism? America floundering into the seventies might well attend to both topics.

Obviously, Lawrence's *Studies in Classic American Literature* is a book, as Pavese's scattered efforts, however gathered, can never be. Lawrence wrote it as a book with powerfully concentrated ulterior motives toward English literature and his own place in it. Pavese's American essays are more fugitive and more desperately achieved: he translated eleven American and four English books (at least; bibliographical data are still sparse), and many of the essays in the present collection are prefaces to them. From 1931 (Sinclair Lewis, *Our Mr. Wrenn*) to 1942 (William Faulkner, *The Hamlet*) Pavese was elbow-deep in a word-for-word scramble with actual texts in a foreign language. Is it surprising that Pavese demonstrates a greater humility before his texts than Lawrence? Just as much as Lawrence, Pavese used his ancillary career as a translator and as an American critic to promote a literary climate at home more hospitable to his own creative effort. But as the overriding value of Pavese's effort was what we might call the hard-core wonder of everyday reality, it was one and the same thing to harass official Italian culture, to prepare the way for his own literary fortunes, and to secure a hearing for the new American voices which obsessed his ear and imagination. Is it surprising, in view of Pavese's long labors in the mills of translation, that he should have used American culture to define for his own culture (and so, now, back to our culture) the hard-core wonder of everyday reality in terms of a new expressive language? By poetry he meant simply the full truth of art, where medium and form and meaning are one.

Pavese's attitude toward American writing is therefore best approached indirectly through his attitude toward writing in general, of which the most eloquent expression is doubtless found in the "Foreword" to *Dialogues With Leucò:*

Had it been possible, I would gladly have done without all this mythology. But myth, it seems to me, is a language of its own, an instrument of expression. There is nothing arbitrary about it. It is a seedbed of symbolic forms, possessing, like all languages, its own range of meanings which can be conveyed in no other way. When we retell an old myth—a proper name, an action, a heroic feat—we are expressing, with the utmost economy of means, a general and comprehensive fact, a core of reality which quickens and feeds a whole organic growth of passion and human existence, an entire conceptual complex. If this mythical name or action also happens to be familiar to us from childhood, from our schooldays, so much the better. What is more acutely disturbing than to see familiar stories troubled into new life? . . . At all costs I wanted to avoid whatever is shapeless, irregular, accidental; even in subject matter, I wanted to confine myself within a given frame; I have tried for a concrete, finite presence. A true revelation, I am convinced, can only emerge from stubborn concentration on a single problem. I have nothing in common with experimentalists, adventurers, with those who travel in strange regions. The surest, and the quickest, way for us to arouse the sense of wonder is to stare, unafraid, at a single object. Suddenly—miraculously—it will look like something we have never seen before.[1]

(It sounds like Thoreau.) A couple of years later, Pavese retold to himself in his diary a comparable discovery about American literature:

The discovery you made in '38 that the message of the Americans is the sense of a mysterious reality underlying the words (cf. the preface to *Alice Toklas*) is true, but must be extended to cover the period of Emerson, Hawthorne, Melville and Whitman. At that time you attributed it to Anderson, Stein and so on. This shows how authentic was the revival of 1916, taking up again the great national theme. A new sense of American democracy considered as a means of enlightenment. The man who is free discovers cosmic reality—a harmony between things and the spirit, a play of symbols transfiguring the things of daily life and giving them a value, a significance, without which the world would be reduced to a skeleton.[2]

I have said that Pavese lacked system (but not coherence). He admired it in others, as long as it derived from the facts of the case and the necessity of the person stating the case. Typically, he wrote Elio Vittorini about the latter's systematic interpretation of American literature (the notes for the famous

1. Trans. William Arrowsmith and D. S. Carne-Ross (Ann Arbor, 1965).
2. *The Burning Brand: Diaries 1935–1950,* trans. A. E. Murch (with Jeanne Molli), (New York, 1961), p. 332. 8 January 1949. In Italian the diaries are published as *Il Mestiere di Vivere* (Turin: Einaudi, 1952).

anthology *Americana*—naturally suppressed by the regime; published years later, in part, in *Diario in Pubblico*):

> During the ten years I have been studying that literature I have not yet come across a synthesis so accurate and so illuminating. I want to tell you this, because it is certain that when your notes become generally known in the world, in your *Short History of Poetical Culture in America,* someone is sure to jump up and say that they are highly original, yes, but fantastic. Now, it should be widely proclaimed that it is precisely because they form a narrative, a novel if you like, that they are so illuminating. I leave aside the justice of the individual criticisms, arrived at by so many intimate and most informative monographs, and I will speak of the play of your theme, the drama of corruption, purity, ferocity and innocence you have established in this history. It is neither by chance nor by choice that you begin with abstract ravings, since your *Conversation in Sicily* had the same (unspoken) conclusion. In this sense it is a great thing that you have conveyed the same tension, the same excited cries of discovery, in your poetical history. Consequently, this work is not concerned with chasing clouds but with a challenging comparison with world literature (that world literature which is implicit, in its entirety, in American literature, if I understand you clearly?). The result is that a century and a half of American literature is reduced to essential evidence of a legend that we have all lived through and which you now relate. . . . In fifty pages you have written a great book. I do not wish to flatter you, but for you I feel the same sense of appreciation that Dante must have had for *De Vulgari:* a literary history seen by a poet as a history of his own poetical feeling.[3]

The tribute equally illuminates Pavese's American criticism, which was also scholarly, personal, narrative, essential, and worldwide.

3. *The Burning Brand,* p. 225. 27 May 1942. The sentence about *Conversation in Sicily* is incorrectly translated, and should read something like this: "It is neither an accident nor an arbitrary act of will that it begins with the abstract furies [see the opening sentence of Vittorini's novel], since its conclusion is, implicitly, the *Conversation in Sicily.*" The comparison to Dante is better rendered ". . . for you it has the significance and the value that the *De Vulgari* must have had for Dante." Pavese's letter (in Italian) also appears in *Lettere 1924–1944,* ed. Lorenzo Mondo (Turin: Einaudi, 1966), p. 634.

It is amazing how much ground he covered, from studies in depth of Whitman and Melville to Gertrude Stein and Faulkner. And clearly he knew well a host of writers—Poe, Hawthorne, Thoreau, Mark Twain, Henry Adams, Henry James, London, Eliot, Hemingway—which he never translated nor discussed at length. He was knowledgeably delighted with Van Wyck Brooks, *The Ordeal of Mark Twain;* with an anthology of criticism edited by Mark Schorer, Josephine Miles, and Gordon McKenzie; he even liked the official *History of the United States.* ("Why are not all American books like these?") [4] From Melville to Stein, from O. Henry to Richard Wright, the reach is grand, and only slightly better than the grasp.

It is also true that Pavese—not with complete foresight or intention, I think—was noticeably selective. He not only spread his American subjects but he bunched them. Except for Whitman and Masters, American poetry seldom engaged him, not so much, perhaps, because Pavese was more a novelist than a poet (if he was), or because he didn't know and like the American poets (which he did), or because prose is all that much easier than verse to translate. Pavese's incessantly repeated principle of the whole work's imaginative unity being encapsulated in the single sentence or a line made it quite indifferent whether he thought in terms of narrative or lyric; and indeed one of the most striking Pavesean revelations is the wonderful ease with which he managed to think of them almost interchangeably. The chief cause of his emphasis on prose is surely its greater marketability to a broad public, whether in translation or in critical discourse, the other side of that coin being the clear and present danger of discussing American prose in a literary situation dominated by Mussolini's censors. Pavese, who was otherwise so little political (except in the sense suggested by the quotation at the head of this foreword), throve on the defiance of unauthorized authority.

Despite the chronological spread of the topics, there is a re-

4. Cesare Pavese, *Lettere 1945–1950,* ed. Italo Calvino (Turin, 1966), p. 342. 18 January 1949.

gional and a temporal emphasis. Both are apparent in Pavese's passion for Sherwood Anderson and Edgar Lee Masters. Like any competent American literature man, Pavese was well aware that our nineteenth-century writing was mainly Eastern seaboard, and that our early twentieth-century literary renaissance was mainly Midwestern. In both cases Pavese was devoted to the new. In the final analysis he preferred the twentieth-century Midwesterners because they were less sectional, more deeply national, than the nineteenth-century Easterners. Aside from an occasional raid on the American heartland in support of his own quite different Piedmontese regionalism, his passionate ambivalent identification with his own *paese,* what excited Pavese about the American Midwest was not so much its actualities, about which he can be scathing, as its imaginative "centrality." It must always be remembered that Pavese never visited or lived in America, that America was for him a foreign country, although a shifting and sliding special case. He had no stake in its sectional chauvinisms. He had a vital stake in its whole literature because, as his letter to Vittorini makes clear, he had a stake in the literature of the whole world. For a while, America seemed to him the probable center of that whole, so that this center was a matter of considerable consequence, realistic and mythic at once. The center was where things were happening in the world of the mind; it was where the future was being born and licked into shape; it was simultaneously Turin and Chicago. From the two Pavese could triangulate his literary universe, the universal, local, and new poetic language of an ever more deeply and precisely defined humanity.

The careless reader must not be misled by the fact that Pavese writes better than most American critics (supposing that at least some of his stylistic merit survived translation) into thinking him an armchair essayist or journalistic impressionist. He wrote literary criticism as if it were a narrative art; he also wrote it as a literary critic. Having once been asked for a piece not excessively critical, Pavese tartly replied that he would be absolutely incapable of writing a page not "excessively critical." [5] Of a slovenly work whose structure (one of Pavese's literary gods, along with auctorial unity, and linguistic reality) was not readily discernible, he demanded: "Where is the fable, where is the myth, where is the symbol, where is the reality?" [6] The terms are closely concatenated. Of another volume which he rejected for the publishing house of Einaudi, he remarked that it was pleasant reading, "but it has no methodological seriousness. . . . How can one live without methodological seriousness"? [7] Pavese could not.

In minor matters—exact quotation, correct dates, titles, page numbers, and the like—he was often cavalier. In major matters he was surprisingly professional and even academic. He began his working life as a teacher in a *liceo,* and he never gave up the scholar's ideals. In an early (1931) uncollected review of a French Whitman anthology ("Walt Whitman in France"), Pavese already reveals his reluctance to write a piece not "excessively critical." His attack on the stale and slipshod work (stale and slipshod by French standards) is not only severely unfavorable but closely detailed, and it succinctly shows his aspirations and criteria, together with the woeful condition of American studies in Italy in 1931. Pavese's positive terms of emphasis are "science," "method," "serious and organized research," "interpretation"—in short, the deliberate and deliberative use of the intellect, precisely what we should expect of a countryman of Dante's. It is from this direction, historically and realistically, that we should come to Pavese's American criticism, rather than by reasoning our way backward to it from his later fiction.

Fifteen years after "Walt Whitman in France," Pavese wrote a long review of F. O. Matthiessen's *American Renaissance.* The essay begins with Pavese playing the role of the naive Ital-

5. *Lettere 1924–1944,* p. 365. June (?) 1933.
6. *Lettere 1945–1950,* p. 147. 5 August 1947.
7. *Ibid.,* p. 264. 26 June 1948.

ian reader, surprised by the news that the great American renaissance of the twentieth century was neither the first nor the greatest literary flowering in American history. Pavese, with his roots deep in Melville and Whitman, of course knew better, even though he surprisingly dated his "discovery" of the relation of the two periods at 1938 (in that previously quoted passage from his diary). At one point Pavese quotes his old (1933) essay on Whitman as evidence that he had said much earlier a lot of what Matthiessen was saying now. Indeed, *American Renaissance* was just such a study as Pavese had implicitly demanded in "Walt Whitman in France," for the war had constrained Americans also to take the self-conscious backward look, "accustoming many American brains to rethink their own past, to question it about the present and about the future: in brief, to make history of it." Pavese had used virtually the same language to praise French scholarship as distinct from Italian. "They make a history, in short, of this literature."

In Matthiessen's *storia* Pavese found little to quarrel with, and naturally so, for although they were born to different cultures, in respect of place and politics, they had both been called to live in the same literary world, the creative discovery of the New World past as a means for propelling the American, and the Italian, and indeed the whole world present toward ever-greater prospects of civilized renewal. Pavese reveled in Matthiessen's critical method, rejoicing in the way an upstart American was giving the age-old Italians a lesson; apparently he failed to notice Matthiessen's tacit admission (in "Method and Scope") that his most serious critical principles were derived from Croce and De Sanctis. The rather Crocean Pavese also reveled in Matthiessen's emphasis upon a realistic and living American language, "the social functionality of expression, the identification of the word with the thing represented, and the inevitability of symbolism." Pavese had long been intrigued with similar verbal qualities in Sherwood Anderson, Edgar Lee Masters, John Dos Passos, and he had already traced the origins of these verbal qualities to the age of Melville and Whitman. Again and again, in the twentieth-century essays, Pavese returns to nineteenth-century American conditions of literature or life for explanations. Much as he admired certain younger writers, such as Dos Passos, who showed what modern America was really like, Pavese clearly preferred the elder moderns—Lewis, Masters, and especially Anderson—who showed him how modern America came to be. These writers, together with Gertrude Stein, Dreiser, and even O. Henry, are all conspicuously transitional between the American Renaissance and the age of Faulkner and Eliot.

In fact, Pavese rather disliked American writers more nearly contemporary with himself (especially expatriates), and one way of explaining why his American dream came to an end would be to say that modern American literature finally caught up with him. How fast the dream faded can be measured by the spiritual distance between the review of Matthiessen in 1946 and "A Negro Speaks to Us," a radio talk on Richard Wright which Pavese delivered the following year. "A Negro Speaks to Us" opens with a historical retrospect that sounds harmless enough, except perhaps for the ambiguously ominous first sentence: "The times in which we discovered America are finished. In the course of a decade, from 1930 to 1940, Italy not only made the acquaintance of at least half a dozen contemporary American writers whose names will remain, but also dug up again some of the nineteenth-century classics of that literature and glimpsed the radical continuity that runs under all the past and present manifestations of that people." Then the tone darkens. Pavese had praised Matthiessen's historical and critical research; here he complains that "the truly important books which now come to us from beyond the ocean are no longer fiction or poetry but books of history, of interpretation, of comment." As early as 1932, in an uncollected review of Carlo Linati, *Scrittori anglo-americani d'oggi,* Pavese was objecting to the American writers (Pound, Eliot, and even the Italian-American writer Emanuele Carnevali) who came to Europe to "corrupt," or *sfalsare,* themselves. Now he glumly predicts that "for several decades nothing more will come from that people comparable to the names and revelations that enthused our prewar youth." For a man of Pavese's skeptical temper, it seems a strangely unguarded prophecy, and the reasoning behind it equally untypical of Pavese's usual lucidity: "After the war and the occupation, after having long sojourned and conversed among us, the young Americans have undergone an interior process of Europeanization, and have lost a great part of that exotic and tragic candor that was their destiny." For the American dream to remain dreamlike, the Yankees had to stay home. More importantly, Pavese's American dream of literature was to a considerable degree an antipathetic function of the Italy in which he grew up; when that Italy collapsed, he had no further need for the dream, and consequently he often fell into nostalgic petulance.

The battleground of Pavese's literary youth was rapidly receding into the past. In "A Negro Speaks to Us" he dates the period of discovery as "a decade, from 1930 to 1940," but in "Yesterday and Today," three months later, it has shrunk to "around" 1930. Pavese could still be brilliant on the continuity of American literature:

> Those who didn't limit themselves to flipping the pages of a dozen or so startling books that issued from beyond the ocean during those years, but shook the tree to make it drop its hidden fruit also and then searched all around to discover its roots, were soon persuaded that the expressive wealth of that people was born not so much from an obvious search for scandalous and ultimately superficial social assumptions, but from a severe and already century-old desire to compress ordinary experience in language, without there being anything left over. From this motive sprang their continuing effort to readjust language to the new reality of the world, in order to create, in effect, a *new* language, down-to-earth and symbolic, that would justify itself solely in terms of itself and not in terms of any traditional complacency. And of this style which, often vulgarized, still in the latest books surprised us by its unusual clarity, it was not difficult to discover initiators and pi-

oneers in the poet Walt Whitman and in the narrator Mark Twain, who belong to the nineteenth century.

But then paradise was lost again, and Pavese didn't quite know how. On the one hand, he argues (not for the first time) "that American culture has lost its mastery, its innocent and knowing intensity that put it in the vanguard of our intellectual world. Nor can I but remark that the loss coincides with the end, or suspension, of its fight against Fascism." On the other hand, Pavese implies that America never *had* been (as he once so fondly thought) "the gigantic theater where with greater freedom than elsewhere the drama of all was being acted out," and that now, after the war, with the end of censorship, "we learned that many countries in Europe, and in the rest of the world, are today the laboratory where forms and styles are being created." The confusion was not Pavese's alone, it is endemic in European-American relations. The basic question is as ever whether America is a different kind of country, as Pavese had perhaps at first too easily assumed, or, as he bitterly concluded, only another country. Like most Europeans, Pavese tended to think of the United States as a young nation, overlooking the fact that the United States, with all its democratic achievements in life and letters, and all its antidemocratic crimes, antedated European Fascism by approximately a century and a half. "Yesterday and Today": the essay was well titled.

A brief glance at the table of contents immediately reveals the lopsided shape of Pavese's American career. Despite many continuities, there were in effect two careers, here represented as Part One (1930–1934) and Part Two (1938–1950), with a huge hiatus between them. In the spring of 1935, Pavese's favorite literary outlet, *La Cultura,* of which he had recently been acting editor, was suppressed by the regime, and Pavese (together with most of his intellectual circle) was arrested for ill-defined clandestine activities, imprisoned in Turin and Rome, convicted without a real trial, and exiled *al confino* of a small seaside town, Brancaleone, Calabria, as far from Turin as it was possible to be sent and still kept in Italy. Pavese's three-year sentence was later reduced to about seven months, during which period, and for some time afterward, he naturally wrote no more provoking essays about American literature. On the surface, the urban intellectual spent his time merely fighting death by boredom. Beneath the surface, he was undergoing a creative revolution.

By page count, Part One contains over three-quarters of Pavese's American criticism; the remaining quarter is scattered over a period of a dozen years. What happened at Brancaleone? Several things, some good, some bad. A few months out of confinement, Pavese noted in his diary that among the signs warning him that youth was over, the most striking was his loss of interest in literature; [8] this was not literally true, nor is this the first recorded instance of a kind of withdrawal which ultimately led to the suicide of 1950, and in fact a few months earlier Pavese had written in his diary that "to suffer an injustice gives one a bracing shock." [9] Glancing far backward, Pavese said that in the clandestine period (Part One) "all was hope," whereas "now"—well after the end of the war—"all is a prospective of disaster." [10] Meanwhile in Brancaleone Pavese was meditating and plotting a move from poetry into fiction. His first period was thus the simultaneous discovery of America and the mastery of a poetic world. His second period was the prose elaboration of the poetic world, for which America was no longer much needed, until it suddenly resurfaced, as summary climax, more topic than inspiration, and decidedly negative, in *The Moon and the Bonfires,* at the tag end of his life. "This search for a new starting point is linked with a craze for construction." [11] Yes, but not so simply as some of Pavese's interpreters have supposed. To get from Pavese's

8. *The Burning Brand,* p. 59. 13 September 1936.
9. *Ibid.,* p. 52. 24 April 1936.
10. *Ibid.,* p. 305. 5 April 1947.
11. *Ibid.,* p. 33. 9 November 1935.

Americanist passions to his novels it is necessary to go through his poetry, and then to understand why his allegedly Americanized fictions—Pavese persistently argued that they weren't American, and I tend to agree—are congruent with a lapsing interest in American literature, and indeed with an increasingly irritable rejection of it. There are lovely pieces in Part Two—the preface to "Benito Cereno," for example—but the great work clearly belongs to the early period of poetic discovery. More closely considered, the great work was over with the Whitman essay of 1933, which doubtless drew heavily on the earlier university thesis, and it began only in 1930 with the long critique of Sinclair Lewis. The dates of publication are separated by three years less a couple of months.

The early years were intense, communal, and in some ways as idyllic as the early essays on Lewis and Anderson. Pavese was writing for the group of older intellectuals who published *La Cultura* and who welcomed his American contributions to it; he was also working with the close international help of an Italian-American friend, Antonio Chiuminatto (eventually professor of music at St. Thomas College in Minnesota). Chiuminatto sent Pavese books, unscrambled American idioms, translated slang, read and criticized Pavese's drafts, and even tried, unsuccessfully, to get a couple of the early essays published in American periodicals. For about two years—June 1930 through July 1932—Pavese made vigorous efforts to get to America, most of them in connection with a teaching position at Columbia University which kept looming vaguely and then finally disappeared in a spirit-spout of bureaucracy.

Even a brief glance at the dates of publication (below) suggests the intensity of Pavese's production. He was incessantly reading, translating, reviewing, studying, writing criticism. He rushed from one project to the next, and often kept several going at once, with all the carefree abandon of youth. At the time of Pavese's translation of *Moby-Dick*—widely regarded as untranslatable—he was twenty-four. Returned home from

Brancaleone, he would seem to refer to this entire early period as well as the moment of notation: "Of the two things, writing poetry and studying, it is the second that gives me greater and more constant comfort. However, I do not forget that my pleasure in studying is always with a view to writing poetry. But, fundamentally, writing poetry is an ever-open wound whence the health-giving lifeblood drains away." [12] Already, at Brancaleone, he had written that his work "draws its sustenance from the strongest roots, national and traditional; it strives to keep its eyes on world trends in literature, and has been particularly aware of literary experiments and achievements in North America, where at one time I thought I had discovered an analogous development. Perhaps the fact that American culture no longer interests me in the least, means that I have outgrown this Piedmontese point of view. I think it does; at any rate, the viewpoint I have had hitherto." [13] It was a long way from 1929 when Pavese had committed himself to study exhaustively American literature: *io intendo darmi a fondo allo studio della letteratura americana.*[14] A year later, citing his just-published essay on Lewis and his soon-to-be-published essay on Anderson, he described himself as one who had been dedicating himself to English and American literature for several years, *da più anni.*[15] The dedication was deep, dramatic, and brief. Again like Thoreau, Pavese had other lives to lead. The present collection makes one of them available to his temporarily adopted compatriots and ongoing heirs.

Pavese's major literary essays, published and unpublished, were posthumously collected, arranged, and edited by his younger friend Italo Calvino in a volume entitled *La letteratura americana e altri saggi.*[16] I have included all the American essays (and four English essays in an appendix), but I

12. *Ibid.,* p. 41. 29 December 1936.
13. *Ibid.,* p. 28. 11 October 1935.
14. *Lettere 1924–1944,* p. 161. 29 November 1929.
15. *Ibid.* p. 254. 25 November 1930.
16. Turin: Einaudi, 1951.

have departed from Calvino's arrangement of them. The American essays are now in chronological order, and I have restored Pavese's original titles. Where titles were lacking, I have supplied purely descriptive ones, for example, "Additions to the Second Preface to *Moby-Dick*." In the Italian edition, all the essays on a single writer were placed together, and certainly it is instructive to observe what Pavese added to the *Moby-Dick* preface the second time around. The reader who wishes to make the observation may turn from one to the other, for they are plainly labeled. It is also worth bearing in mind that between these two occasions Pavese wrote about Anderson, O. Henry, Dos Passos, Dreiser, Whitman, Faulkner, Gertrude Stein, and did a few more translations from the American and English.

As there are two estimable merits in a translation, elegance and accuracy, so there have always been two chief schools of translators, those desirous of writing well in their own language and those desirous of hewing to the foreign text. I have erred on the side of scrupulosity as far as I could and as much as I dared. I have kept a considerable number of Pavese's inordinately complex sentence structures, and also a considerable number of his sentence fragments; both forms are an essential part of his thought, and not mere garments of thought. I have kept much contorted idiom and eccentric vocabulary—as long as they were penetrable—rather than invent my own standard (or eccentric) English equivalents, hoping thereby to permit a sufficient passage of intelligence to the English reader while at the same time involving him at the nearest possible remove with the text he presumably hopes to approach. Pavese's chaotic paragraphing (which may, in certain instances, be an editor's) appeared to be no transferable form of his thought, and I have not hesitated to cut and restitch it to conventional English patterns.

The quotations from American and English writers in *La letteratura americana e altri saggi* are naturally all in Italian. In their place I have substituted reputable English originals (normally from first editions or recent, definitive scholarly editions). Footnotes are all Pavese's—unless indicated by brackets.

The original provenance of Pavese's American (and English) essays—their first publication in Italian—is as follows:

"An American Novelist, Sinclair Lewis," *La Cultura,* November 1930.
"Sherwood Anderson," *La Cultura,* April 1931.
"The *Spoon River Anthology,*" *La Cultura,* November 1931.
"Herman Melville," *La Cultura,* January–March 1932.
"Preface to *Moby-Dick,*" trans. Pavese. Turin: Frassinelli, 1932.
"Preface to *Dark Laughter,* trans. Pavese. Turin: Frassinelli, 1932.
"O. Henry; or, The Literary Trick," *La Nuova Italia,* 10 March 1932.
"John Dos Passos and the American Novel," *La Cultura,* January–March 1933.
"Dreiser and his Social Battle," *La Cultura,* April–June 1933.
"Interpretation of Walt Whitman, Poet," *La Cultura,* July–September 1933.
"Faulkner, A Bad Pupil of Anderson," *La Cultura,* April 1934.
"The Fictionalized Biographies of Sinclair Lewis," *La Cultura,* May 1934.

"Preface to *The Autobiography of Alice B. Toklas,*" trans. Pavese. Turin: Einaudi, 1938.
"Preface to 'Benito Cereno,'" trans. Pavese. Turin: Einaudi, 1940.
"Preface to *Three Lives,*" trans. Pavese. Turin: Einaudi, 1940.
"Additions to the Second Preface to *Moby-Dick,*" trans. Pavese. Turin: Frassinelli, 1941.
"The Dead at Spoon River," *Il Saggiatore,* 10 August 1943.
"American Ripeness," *La Rassegna d'Italia,* December 1946.
"A Useful Book," *L'Unità* (Turin), 9 March 1947.
"A Negro Speaks to Us," radio review broadcast in May 1947.
"Yesterday and Today," *L'Unità* (Turin), 3 August 1947.
"The Great American Anguish," *L'Unità* (Turin), 12 March 1950.

"Preface to Defoe, *Moll Flanders,*" trans. Pavese. Turin: Einaudi, 1938.

"Preface to Dickens, *David Copperfield,*" trans. Pavese. Turin: Einaudi, 1939.
"Preface to Conrad, *'Twixt Land and Sea.*" Unpublished. Dated in typescript 28 August 1946.
"Robert Louis Stevenson," *L'Unità* (Rome), 27 June 1950.

My chief acknowledgment of indebtedness and gratitude is to Mario Materassi, a young Florentine Americanist who for many hours checked the translation with me, word by word through two languages, idea by idea through two cultures. I also want to thank Erich Linder for assistance in securing translation rights; Paveseans Donald Heiney and R. W. Flint for generous encouragement and correspondence; Mary Burton for help in copyreading and styling; and the editors of the University of California Press for patience, handholding, and faith.

EDWIN FUSSELL

La Jolla, California
4 July 1969

Contents

PART ONE: 1930–1934

PART TWO: 1938–1950

Part One: 1930–1934

AN AMERICAN NOVELIST, SINCLAIR LEWIS

The Americans have invented a new way of drinking. I speak, of course, of a literary way. A character, at a certain point in a novel, throws over everything: good manners, job, family (when he has one), and alone, or accompanied by a bosom friend, he disappears for some time on the usual expedition. "He has gone on the grand sneak." Sometimes the absence lasts for days. In the meantime, the rebel's course is quite simple: from an uproar of songs and bright remarks to an anguished and thoughtful countenance. At the end, the character returns to his place in life. He is a little hung over and wilted, but he has a new awareness of himself; the machinery of civilization does not entirely possess him, life is still worth living. Thus it happens in the novels. (I am not at the moment concerned with how it happens in real life.) And certainly it is a novelty. After the classical banquets, after the satanic debauches of the moderns, our industrial civilization had to create a third way.

America has always been a land of exceptional drinkers. But it is not important here to cite, as usual, Poe, who in any event drank like a European. Not even O. Henry fits the case, the picturesque O. Henry with his happy-go-lucky swindlers and eccentrics, vagabonds through all the states of the Union and beyond, dionysiac and comical drunkards, all of them people who even when in prison (which often happens) seek no release in wine because their spirits are already too gay and free to need it. These people drink, in short, as they breathe. The origins of the new meaning of the paradise of alcohol in contemporary American literature must be sought rather in certain works of the early years of the century, of socialist and revolutionary tendency, in certain novels, for example, by Jack London. Those atrocious benders that Martin Eden indulges with his friend from the laundry in Oakland have for their precise and admitted intention to drug the muscles and intoxicate the spirit, stupefied by brute labor. It is already a protest against a social system which suffocates and denies life. Born as polemic, with the exaggeration and artistic rigidity of all polemic creations, this myth will perpetuate itself in subsequent literature, less bound by ideological preoccupations and more rich in poets. Let two suffice, Sherwood Anderson and Lewis.

They are not exceptional types, these drinkers, but clerks, laborers, journalists, common people, everyday people. They have no furious genius to placate, they are not damned. They are poor men, slaves of the "job," who sometimes resort to this last pretense of individual rebellion. And they never do so in order to commit an outrage; with the same motive, the more refined among them go to hear a concert. Among us nothing like this has ever been written. If in some social novel of the last century a European drinks more than usual, we are in the presence of the usual polemic implication: the drunkard is a worker, a brute, the human beast. The novelty and value of the American myth is that instead the drinker is not at all unusual, but is an average man among men, whose life oppresses him, and he protests in this way. And this submissive rebellion is more tragic than any amount of exemplary satanism or brutalization. Sinclair Lewis—we will see how—describes this world.[1]

1. Of the novels by Sinclair Lewis, there are accessible to Italians in the Tauchnitz editions: *Our Mr. Wrenn, Babbitt,* and *Arrow-*

Meanwhile, his early novels preserve traces of the preponderantly pamphleteering kind of writing of Upton Sinclair and Frank Norris. A certain passion for throwing light on social problems reappears, refined and made art, in the pages of these novels—*The Job, Main Street*[2]—and the situation of Martin Eden, a manual worker and intellectual in love with a daughter of the upper middle class, who teaches him to teach himself, is found again, at several points, in at least two of these novels, *The Trail of the Hawk* and *Free Air.*[3] But with this comparison I do not mean to imply that all Lewis' characters spend their time getting drunk. Anyhow, not even Jack London's characters do. Drinking is virtually a symbol. More precisely, all Lewis' protagonists are melancholy rebels who in a thousand ways—falling in love, living in the open air, changing jobs, studying, going in for art, speaking a many-colored dialect, or even, sometimes, getting plastered—try to escape the humiliating daily grayness, the wearisome vacuity of factories, offices, and homes. They drink, in fact, with an effort, these good Americans, even in the late novels, after 1919, when the obstacle of the Eighteenth Amendment should have made its infraction irresistible and fascinatingly seditious. To Lewis, drunkenness is disgusting, no doubt about it, although in *Our Mr. Wrenn,* in *Babbitt,* and in *Elmer Gantry,* he describes it with a certain flair and an easygoing tolerance.

Ultimately, the thirst of these characters is for one thing only: freedom, freedom for the individual confronted by the irrational restraints of society. It is the national malady of America, a country, if ever there was one, of impertinent mor-

---

smith. Of the others, I have by me the following editions: *The Trail of the Hawk* (London: Jonathan Cape, 1923); *The Job* and *The Innocents* (New York and London: Harper and Brothers, 1917); *Free Air* (1919), *Main Street* (1920), *Mantrap* (1926), *Elmer Gantry* (1927), *The Man Who Knew Coolidge* (1928), and *Dodsworth* (1929) (all from New York: Harcourt, Brace and Company).

2. "Main Street" is the name that in the small towns of the pioneers was usually given to the central road along which the principal buildings were disposed—drugstore, bank, post office, grocery, etc.—and from which branched off little side roads open to the prairie.

3. One should note, in *Free Air,* the double sense of "free," which means "libero" and "gratis."

alists; but not, let it be understood, of supermen—poor creatures, rather, even when they possess genius. Here is the whole novelty of Lewis. From the affability of Wrenn (*Our Mr. Wrenn*), himself a would-be comic playwright as well as a romantic traveler, to the tragedy of Gottlieb (*Arrowsmith*), an exacting and lonely scientist, the Lewis character is always a man among men, stifled by petty miseries and gladdened by modest joys, dreamer of an ideal not always very well defined. And the author views him in an infinite variety of ways which constitute the whole range of his poetry: from grotesque caricature to resigned and thoughtful seriousness.

The richness and the variety of Lewis' world reside in the innumerable attitudes with which he contemplates the spectacle of the daily human revolt against environment and self. And the spectacle makes him smile. In their insatiable timidity, men are comical. And the environment that oppresses them is both comical and grotesque. But sometimes, by virtue of a rebel who acts more seriously than the others or who reflects the common aspirations in a more universal way, the scene becomes tragic. Still, these outbursts of anguish are not the knowing contrivances of a contrapuntal novelist: sometimes, even (in *Elmer Gantry*), they destroy the harmony of the work. The author of *Babbitt* always begins with an amused and mocking tone. Usually he wants to make of all the characters a series of whimsical little men and women, slightly ridiculous, slightly sad. He does not want to have the naive air of taking such types seriously; but every so often it happens, and, in *Main Street,* in *The Job,* everywhere, he comes out with more heartfelt sentences, he contradicts himself, he believes, and he admires. For plainly he himself is the rebel described and all his character types are only the innumerable faces of his ego. Thus it happens that he smiles and laughs, but always in the end caresses the victim with his sorrowful glance. For this reason, as we shall see, *Babbitt* turned out to be the masterpiece: in him, better than in any other character, Lewis fused the preposterous puppet with the human brother whom we must feel sorry for.

Sinclair Lewis is himself the rebel portrayed in the novels. The little man who suffocates and pants for air and doesn't even know what he wants or where he is going, or rather, continually discovers new avenues but argues and struggles with himself, perpetually in flight, is of course the figure of himself which we are permitted to glimpse between the lines. A curious phenomenon of his books illustrates this instability of his spirit: all the human types and backgrounds which in one place he ridicules he elsewhere delights in, he approves of them, he is moved by them. For example, the situation of the customary city dweller who is going to make an excursion to get close to nature—roughing it, as they say, living and laboring in the open air—occurs twice, at least, in two novels, *Babbitt* and *Mantrap*. In the first, the attempt is viewed gaily, humorously, with typical Paul Riesling, half absorbed and half hysterical. In the second, the trip to Canada is a spiritual victory wherein Ralph Prescott has nothing comical about him, and he even manages, without becoming ridiculous, to wear the moccasins which would yield such comedy on the flabby feet of Babbitt. Gopher Prairie, the town that in *Main Street* Lewis excommunicated and described as not only grotesque but unbearable in its vulgarity, becomes in *Free Air* an interesting Western stopover where even the traveling salesmen are sympathetically treated. And the drinking that in *Arrowsmith* is practically acceptable in the emigrants of St. Hubert, who think they are now going home, is revolting in Eddie Schwirtz in *The Job*.

All these uncertainities of judgment which, in any case, ought to be gratefully accepted, since with them our author has multiplied the variety of his situations, are reflected in the last and most comprehensive uncertainty of all, that uncertainty through which Sinclair Lewis, the most knowing expert of slang and the American vernacular [4] now writing in the

4. The difference between "slang" and colloquial American is well known: the former is practically a jargon, a pepper pot of grotesque metaphors and pungent expressions, a creation, in short, conscious, deliberate, and applauded except by the most cultivated, the purists;

United States, and the first and most determined to derive from it artistic results, condemns, in effect, his own glory, making slang the characteristic of his most vulgar personages and calling attention to the fact: "slangy" and "backslapping" are the attributes of Schwirtz (*The Job*) and Schmaltz (*The Man Who Knew Coolidge*). But gradually this conventional judgment fades before the down-to-earth quality of the man's nature and origins, before his irresistible passion for the genuine and the powerful, and he ends in the creation of two superb figures, sturdy and full-blooded, sympathetic though theatrical, who are also, to return to our starting point, great drinkers: G. Sondelius (*Arrowsmith*) and Elmer Gantry, of whom I shall speak again.

Sinclair Lewis achieved fame with *Main Street* (1920). This interminable novel—where the ennui that suffocates the soul of the heroine, buried in the vulgarity and gossip of a small Minnesota town, ends, through the static quality of the characters and the monotony of Carol's reactions, in suffocating the soul of the reader as well—is the work that brought fame to the author of *Babbitt*. Even *Babbitt* (1922): I swear that all that uproar is caused more by its social quality, its satire of a class (the average American businessman), and by the great and noisy gaiety of the characters' conversations, than by the more essential values of art. *Main Street* is not, however, an example of something taking hold with the customarily stupid public (everybody knows how stupid the public is, and neither you nor I are part of it), but this time—what a coincidence!—it made a great hit with the author. Sinclair Lewis was convinced that in *Main Street* he had written a great

---

colloquial American, on the other hand, is simply the great body of the language spoken in the United States, different from English as phonetics and morphology, often as vocabulary, and nearly always as construction: the changed conditions of the English settlers, contacts with settlers from other peoples, natural evolution, and "slang" have contributed to its formation. Cf. Henry L. Mencken, *The American Language* (2d ed., New York, 1921).

work, his great work, which he had cherished—if one may believe his critic and biographer, Charles C. Baldwin—for at least fifteen years. It was a tale minutely realistic, a background new or almost new, under that aspect, to the national literature; and, at the same time, it was a courageous attack on a frame of mind still dominant. All must applaud. Gopher Prairie, Minnesota, was a photographic likeness—too much of a likeness—and, according to the author's intention, it stood for hundreds of Gopher Prairies, it stood for all America. From the novel a film was even made by Warner Brothers. And the habit of describing a man and a setting representative of a class, of an intellectual phase, of a profession, would persist in Lewis in such a way that it would on other occasions lead him into sin. Sinclair Lewis, as Baldwin also says, wrote *Free Air* (1919), the novel immediately preceding the story of Carol, in order to get the money that would allow him to attend to *Main Street.* It is the usual mischance that happens to writers: *Free Air,* this *nuga,* is a jewel of poetry in comparison with the gross machine that followed it a year later.

Sinclair Lewis had already written several books in the years between the outbreak of the European war and 1920. This group of novels describes a whole intellectual epoch, and I want to speak of them a little, since almost nothing is known of them in Italy, or, at least, nothing about them appears those few times when the classic *Babbitt* is discussed. With respect to *Babbitt,* the neglect would be no great evil if, in order to treat critically and understandingly a work by a certain writer, this work only sufficed the reader.

Several novels, then, quite different from those which will follow *Main Street: Our Mr. Wrenn* (1914), *The Trail of the Hawk* (1915), *The Job* (1917), *The Innocents* (1917), and *Free Air* (1919). One characteristic that distinguishes them from their successors is that they all have happy endings. By a happy ending I mean a resigned acceptance, a peaceable return to the track which, for the entire novel, the rebel has been trying to jump, or, more often, to a marriage Ibsen-style, rejuvenated and Americanized; the choice of a companion (*The Trail of the Hawk, Free Air, The Job*) with whom to look forward to a future of freedom and struggle. A conclusion, then, this last one, somewhat cinematographic and banal, if it were not for the continuous commentary, malicious and tolerant, with which these pages are adorned, and, more than anything, for the sympathetic and genuine nature of the protagonists, toward whose provincial naiveté the author offers spiritual indulgences, and whose gay and youthful seriousness he brings to birth through intimate sympathy from an indigenous root; all of them are people of the Middle West, as he himself was.

This poetry of young life, enjoyed as a beautiful adventure, bold and simple, extending from its commonplace origins to the conquest of the whole world, is perfect in *Free Air,* the story of the vicissitudes of a restless young man from Schoenstrom, a prairie village in Minnesota, the enterprising and frustrated proprietor of a public garage. He sees an aristocratic couple from Brooklyn going by in an automobile, a young lady who drives and her father who, without too much conviction, seeks in the wide open spaces the health he lost in overwork. The two intend to cross the continent from Minneapolis to Seattle. Milt Daggett, the young man, abandons his business, climbs into his flivver, and follows the girl. Adventures, in which wide-awake, practical Milt Daggett clears away obstacles for the gentlefolk. Boy, does he like the girl! She, in the meantime, is discovering the great body of America, the unsuspected reality of people and of actual life, the fascinating seriousness and freshness of the Midland. In her enthusiasm, she catechizes the young man, who at bottom thinks Shoenstrom will always be an unbearable hole, but who is glad to listen and even to read Vachel Lindsay. He discovers that he is much like the poets (" 'Thought poetry was all . . . rhymed bellyachin' about hard luck' ") , and begins to wonder what kind of life the girl leads in Brooklyn. They arrive at Seattle. Milt, a new Martin Eden, begins to study, in order to make himself worthy. Complications with the young lady's background. And here is how the novel ends (the two are stuck in the mud in a shallow river crossing) :

"If you kiss me again like that, we'll both topple overboard. By the way, *can* we get the car out?"

"I think so, if we put on the chains. We'll have to take off our shoes and stockings."

Shyly, turning from him a little, she stripped off her stockings and pumps, while he changed from a flivver-driver into a young viking, with bare white neck, pale hair ruffled about his head, trousers rolled up above his straight knees—a young seaman of the crew of Eric the Red.

They swung out on the running-board, now awash.

"Watch out for that turn! Heavens, how I have to look after you! Is there a class in cooking at your university? No—do—not—kiss—me—on—a—turn!"

This is the beginning of the story of Milt and Claire Daggett.

The prelude over and the curtain risen on the actual play, they face the anxieties and glories of a changing world. Not without quarrels and barren hours, not free from ignorance and the discomfort of finding that between the mountain peaks they must for long gray periods dwell in the dusty valleys, they yet start their drama with the distinction of being able to laugh together, with the advantage of having discovered that neither Schoenstrom nor Brooklyn Heights is quite all of life, with the cosmic importance to the tedious world of believing in the romance that makes youth unquenchable.

These early Lewis novels are, in fact, idylls, rather slight adventures that have all the popular flavor and the easy and mocking tone of the idyll. *The Trail of the Hawk* is an idyll, with its story of the young man who lives in the open air, at liberty, a jack-of-all-trades, who is born at Joralemon, Minnesota, who goes on to the conquest of the world, and who ends by meeting the usual girl from the upper middle class, the companion, like him suffering from restraints and anxious for freedom and good causes. *The Innocents* is an idyll, the gentle and delightful story of a young-hearted old couple who try to strike out on their own and suffer mishaps, always happy, Father to play the mouth organ, Mother to adore him and to maunder on, two sprightly people who flee like gamins from the tyranny of a daughter who wants them to be old at any cost; and in the end even they regain a position in life.

This tale, and *Our Mr. Wrenn,* another good-natured story about a modest clerk and dreamer of adventures, who takes a trip to Europe and awkwardly and unhappily falls in love there, and then returns to his job and his world of little people and finds in them peace and happiness—the whole thing told with that inimitable tone, which later still will be in part that of *Babbitt,* of indulgent amusement and resigned superiority to the character—these two novels, as I say, *Our Mr. Wrenn* and *The Innocents,* particularly *Our Mr. Wrenn,* are the masterpieces of the idyllic Lewis. Before *Babbitt,* this was Lewis' best work, and it went almost unnoticed, to such an extent that the author, having achieved a fame from which he could revive the book for his readers, reprinted it with others of the early years.

It might be said that in this early novel Lewis had as good as condensed all the poetry that he would subsequently develop, little by little, in the various future works. In the two protagonists of the novel—Mr. Wrenn (already described) and Istra Nash, the art student, eager and tired of life, with whom Wrenn falls in love, a capricious and adorable female, and at the same time an intellectual whom artistic failure and critical acumen have tragically cut off from life—we have the two polar types of Lewis' fictional world. Wrenn we will meet again in Babbitt and in Sam Dodsworth, Istra, divided into two parts, in Leora (*Arrowsmith*), in Alverna (*Mantrap*), and in Sharon Falconer (*Elmer Gantry*), on the one hand, and, on the other, in Paul Riesling (*Babbitt*), in Arrowsmith himself, in Gottlieb (*Arrowsmith*), and in Frank Shallard (*Elmer Gantry*).

Here is a little sample of dialogue from the novel:

"Oh, gee! I just can't get over it—you here by me—ain't it curious! . . ." Then he persisted with the tale of his longing, which she had so carefully interrupted: "The people here are *awful* kind and good, and you can bank on 'em. But—oh——."

From across the room, Tom's pretended jeers, lighted up with Miss Proudfoot's giggles, as paper lanterns illumine Coney Island. From Tom:

"Yes, you're a hot dancer, all right. I suppose you can do the Boston and all them swell dances. Wah-h-h-h-h!"

"——but Istra, oh, gee! you're like poetry—like all them things a feller can't get but he tries to when he reads Shakespeare and all those poets."

"Oh, dear boy, you mustn't."

And this letter, sent by Istra to Paris after her meeting with Wrenn, completes the picture:

Skilly dear, I'm in a fierce Bloomsbury boarding-house—bores—except for a Phe-nomenon—little man of 35 or 40 with embryonic imagination & a virgin soul. I'll try to keep from planting radical thoughts in the virgin soul, but I'm tempted.

Oh Skilly dear I'm lonely as the devil. Would it be too bromid. to say I wish you were here? I put out my hand in the darkness, & yours wasn't there. My dear, my dear, how desolate ——Oh you understand it only too well with your supercilious grin & your superior eye-glasses & your beatific Oxonian ignorance of poor eager America.

I suppose I *am* just a barbarous Californian kiddy. It's just as Pere Duréon said at the atelier, "You haf a' onderstanding of the 'igher immorality, but I 'ope you can cook—paint you cannot."

He wins. I can't sell a single thing to the art editors here or get one single order. One horrid eye-glassed earnest youth who Sees People at a magazine, he vouchsafed that they "didn't use any Outsiders." Outsiders! And his hair was nearly as red as my wretched mop. So I came home & howled & burned Milan tapers before your picture. I did. Though you don't deserve it.

Oh damn it, am I getting sentimental? You'll read this at Petit Monsard over your drip & grin at your poor unnietzschean barbarian.

I.N.

Such is *Our Mr. Wrenn*. It introduces still another aspect of the world I am describing, namely, social controversy. What will become a thesis in *Main Street* appears, in human form, in Wrenn's speeches. Among the many impractical ideas which serve as points of view for the daydreaming clerk, and for his friend Morton, on the cattle boat that is taking them to England, is this, that socialism might become a new religion. These ideas—one time it is socialism in general, another time cooperation, still another time pacifism, the rational upbringing of children, feminism, and so forth—did not always remain opinions of a character. In *The Job* they constitute the novel's thesis—a somewhat sweetened thesis, however, that does not ruin the book, but rather adds poetry to it. In the person of Una Golden, the orphaned protagonist who is trying to give some meaning to existence, these ideas of renewal become her ordeal, stages of her quest, and the author views her with some detachment. Although he concludes by making Una happy in a marriage that will permit her to remake her life toward other ends than merely bearing children, still he never ceases to describe, in human terms, without ulterior motives, some people who show the merit of these doctrines and others who show their ingenuity. *The Job* is a curious novel which miraculously escapes thesis and boredom, thanks to the wide variety of settings it presents: New York offices, New York landscapes, the provincial wonder of Una Golden when she arrives, and her experience of married life with Ed Schwirtz, the first type of the average vulgar man, of the same stuff as the young men from Minnesota, but no longer young and without ever having felt the divine restlessness of those others. This type, incidentally, will continue to haunt Lewis until Babbitt, until Gantry, until *The Man Who Knew Coolidge,* now grotesque, now pathetic, now robust and full of life, the best known, the most frequently remarked, and the least understood among Lewis' creations.

The final couple of this novel, Una and Walter Babson, is the usual couple from the idylls; and just as Una is the usual desperate and overserious seeker after freedom in a new order, so Walter is the usual individual impatient with his job, drinker and pagan, born in the country (this time in Kansas), a man of letters, a perfect Sinclair Lewis, since, as I was forgetting to say, all these young Middle Western revolutionaries are, in many respects, and all too clearly, autobiographical.

With *Main Street,* Lewis set out to show—polemically, fulminating against certain tyrannies imposed upon his youth—that reverse side of the picture of the Middle West that he has been painting ever since. *Main Street* is not badly written. The art of the novel is scrupulously observed. There is characterization, there is setting, there is unity, there are dramatic moments, there is even catharsis. And it brought fame to its author. Still, *Main Street* is boring. It is polemic. It is a long bill of particulars. It is a caricature without a smile. After reading the pages that describe all that moral meanness, we are willing to say: Yes, Sinclair Lewis is right. But Carol's torment, at which the author implacably hammers page after page, for four hundred and fifty pages, in the end tells us nothing further.

As for the things that are more entertaining, after a while we notice that they have nothing to do with the center of the book. There are even characters or situations from the preceding books, Bjornstam, for example, the village atheist and socialist, alter ego of Bone Stillman of Joralemon in *The Trail of the Hawk.* Or (the usual irony) they are not that reverse side of the Middle West at which the author is supposed to be looking, but are instead portraits that in some way still represent and exalt their native land: they are, for example, reflections of the happy-go-lucky tramps, the vagabonds, of *Free Air* and *The Innocents,* Pinky from the former and Crook from the latter. The entire book resembles that stroll which Carol takes by herself, when she arrives at Gopher Prairie, along Main Street and side streets, where the author keeps slipping in tendentious descriptions and remarks on the houses and shops that are seen. The only interesting moment in Carol—after her first appearance, of course—is the change in her spirit following her encounter with Erik Valbord: if she can't succeed in reforming a city, she wants at least to refine a man. This is human, and so is the adventure of Fern Mullins, the scatterbrained young schoolmistress. But nothing else is poetry. It is, as I said, a bill of particulars. And it is boring.

Despite all this, *Main Street* marks a forward step for its author, an intellectual advance although an artistic failure. After it, Sinclair Lewis almost entirely forgets that world of youthful adventure that was so delightful to him, and with it the theoretical happy endings, the generous ideas, the idylls, and the socialistic tirades. He loses that slightly naive faith in existence that in all the novels prior to 1920 used to make him scatter abroad sayings about life, for the sheer fun of it, even when they were disenchanted. One might say that the extended cohabitation with his characters in the limbo of Gopher Prairie had revealed to him a tragedy of existence. His once indulgent smile will be henceforth laughter, sorrowful laughter, and the cheerful eccentrics will become painful grotesques. The imaginative adventures (*The Trail of the Hawk, Free Air*) are struck at the root: even the desire for them becomes ridiculous (*Babbitt*) or melancholy (*Arrowsmith*). The self-reliant young women, cheerful and eager, who used to furnish happy endings to the idylls, now, like the already-mentioned Istra Nash, become unattainable, tortured even when simple; they die halfway through the story, or they go away, all of them desperate images of the author's relentless and henceforth tragic struggle for freedom.

Naturally, it is a great advance with respect to the breadth and resonance of a fictive world, this development suggested by *Main Street*. The characters become ampler and more numerous and more surely drawn. The plots become more exciting through lively contrast, where the Lewis irony still most subtly prevails, sadder now in tone. There remains, there is even increased, a single defect, as I have already said, the mania for undertaking in each novel the portrait of a social class with its background and the treatment of related problems. Of it is born a slight tedium of tone, quite different from that in *Main Street,* but no less wearying. In *Arrowsmith* everything is medicine, in *Elmer Gantry* everything is religion.

I have already said that *Babbitt* (1922) is Lewis' masterpiece because in it the most ridiculous puppet is seen with the most cheerfully hopeless eye possible. But it is inexact to say "puppet." Babbitt affects us precisely because he shows us how being an average man, a common man, a normal man, is like being a puppet. What reader of the novel, while reading it, has not every so often squirmed, asking himself how many times he himself has been a Babbitt?

And, I repeat, the book's greatness lies in the fact that Babbitt is restless, that Babbitt—in this respect more than ever Babbitt—does not want to be a Babbitt, and that all his efforts fail, leaving him terribly resigned, terribly good-natured, and ready to begin again. At a certain point, every cliché, every glad-handing phrase, every gesture, every ridiculous scene—and the reader knows how full of them the book is—becomes a barb which we see stuck in Babbitt, and he doesn't notice, but from it his character emerges, tortured, quite stoic, and still without heroism, the most common—and thus the most extraordinary—martyr the world has ever seen.

It has been said that *Babbitt* is a great work because of its realism, that in it life is photographed, that to hear those big professional men and industrialists from the Middle West is like hearing a phonograph record of American vulgarity. That is not true, or at least it is not the whole truth. *Babbitt* is a paradoxical book. Yes, there is in it material collected by almost superhuman observation, but this is only raw material. In the book there is created a synthesis, a synthesis that is poetry, by means of which all the characters become functions of Babbitt, and by means of which all the characters speak realistically, since it is reality itself which will exasperate and clutch him again; but it is a realism so little realistic and instead so full of poetry that, if for a moment the figure of Babbitt is removed, we can see how all the fragments of that vaunted realism no longer of themselves say anything, how they no longer reflect any reality except (imperfectly) that of the missing hero.

So much for the work of art. As for history, we see in George F. Babbitt fused for the first time—the second time in Sam Dodsworth—two of Lewis' incompatible extremes: the sensitive and timid character, the dreamer, "our Mr. Wrenn," and the coarse and simpleminded Middle Westerner, Eddie Schwirtz. Thanks to a miracle of art, they coexist perfectly in Babbitt.

I don't want to summarize the book. Still, I will observe how this long story of escapes and defeats, until the end, the rebellion, the betrayal to Zenith, which concludes as unhappily as the other novels, has, in its almost journalistic treatment of a slice of life, a fascination that makes up for the possible defect of its lack of construction—in other words—as a novel. Here again, as several times already and other times still to come, Lewis follows a character through a certain period in his life, without organizing the whole into any obvious plot, but telling, as a newspaper reporter would, various adventures, unconnected with each other. Naturally, there is adventure and it is wholly intellectual—a flight, a rebellion, a discovery, a defeat—but the character so portrayed in the midst of daily life has the advantage of remaining more a type, presented to the mind, of being less tied to any particular events, of adapting himself more broadly to the readers' imagination. To see what I mean, think of what Mowgli is in the Jungle Books, in those disparate and isolated adventures that make up the chronicle of his life. He is a symbol that everyone likes to imagine. In the same way we may explain the extraordinary ease with which these types of Lewis' became a part of real life. And Babbitt, for the same reason as Don Quixote, is now better known as a type than as the creation of a poet.

This lust for symbolism may also be seen in the persistence of Zenith—Babbitt's city—in Lewis' world. It is unfortunate, since Zenith was made for Babbitt, as were all the characters and settings of the novel, and when Babbitt is removed they dry up and blow away. Thus in *Arrowsmith,* Lewis invents even the state in which Zenith is located, Winnemac, and gives its boundaries and conditions, and at a certain point Babbitt turns up in his setting, but now the reader is living with memories. Likewise in *Elmer Gantry,* in *The Man Who Knew Coolidge,* in *Dodsworth,* Zenith is a symbol, the American city, as Gopher Prairie was the village; but Zenith is dead.

These novels of the second period, after *Main Street,* might even be called the Zenith novels, except for one, *Mantrap* (1926), which escapes the category. As for art, *Mantrap* contains Alverna, the first of the three magnificent women whom Sinclair Lewis creates in these last books. Alverna is an uncultivated Istra Nash. She is a manicurist whose husband takes her to Canada, where she is bored and runs away. The usual rebellion and an unexpected unhappy ending. All part friends, at last, but each by his own road. And it is still another idyll, of the earlier sort, this adventure all full of the joy of uncivilized life: a lawyer who in Canada becomes a man again, and there gets to know Joe Easter, the husband, a crude type characterized by courtesy and loyalty, and there he courts Alverna, who flirts in a heavenly fashion, and escapes in his company.

Finally, there are *Arrowsmith* (1925) and *Elmer Gantry* (1927). The immediate motive of these two books is obvious: in the first, pitilessly to anatomize the world of medicine and related professions, in the second to do the same for ministers and bigots of every kind. In *Arrowsmith* there are memories of childhood and adolescence (Sinclair Lewis is the son of a country doctor in Minnesota), which also turn up in the pages of university life in *Elmer Gantry.* The chief difference is that Martin Arrowsmith takes seriously what he does whereas Gantry is a charlatan. But one cannot get rid of the two books with this catch phrase, as some critics have done. In a sense,

Elmer Gantry is not a hypocrite, and those who say he is have understood nothing; even if he wants to be one, the issue is much more serious.

Certainly, on an academic reading, *Arrowsmith*—I will glance at the other one later—is a badly made book. It was written hastily, with interruptions, and it lacks construction. But it is one of those badly made novels that you read without stopping and then later you remember eagerly the excessive abundance of life that informs them. The hero is in earnest and is taken earnestly by the author. By now earnest types abound in Lewis. Martin Arrowsmith, this young man from Elk Mills, Winnemac (read Minnesota), looks on life with severe eyes, and all the passion of his youth is devoted to discovering a worthy purpose in the pursuit of science and life. At the university he is restless, without being obstreperous: he doesn't really know what he wants. He has the temperament of the young men of the early novels, but along with it the sad and already defeated countenance of Istra Nash. He is suspended from the university, and behold him, a vagabond:

> Always, in America, there remains from pioneer days a cheerful pariahdom of shabby young men who prowl causelessly from state to state, from gang to gang, in the power of the Wanderlust. They wear black sateen shirts, and carry bundles. They are not permanently tramps. They have home towns to which they return, to work quietly in the factory or the section-gang for a year—for a week—and as quietly to disappear again. They crowd the smoking cars at night; they sit silent on benches in filthy stations; they know all the land yet of it they know nothing, because in a hundred cities they see only the employment agencies, the all-night lunches, the blind-pigs, the scabrous lodging-houses. Into that world of voyageurs Martin vanished. Drinking steadily, only half-conscious of whither he was going, of what he desired to do . . . he flitted from Zenith to the city of Sparta, across to Ohio, up into Michigan, west to Illinois. His mind was a shambles. He could never quite remember, afterward, where he had been. Once, it is clear, he was soda-fountain clerk in a Minnemagantic drugstore. Once he must have been, for a week, dishwasher in the stench of a cheap restaurant. He wandered by freight trains, on blind baggages, on foot. To his fellow prospectors he was

known as "Slim," the worst-tempered and most restless of all their company.

Then he returns and takes his medical degree. He becomes a country doctor in North Dakota, he becomes assistant to the Director of Public Health at Nautilus, Iowa, pathologist in a clinic in Chicago, and finally a research scientist in an institute in New York. He goes out to test his cure against the plague in the West Indies, returns famous, enters high society, is disgusted with it, throws over everything, and withdraws into the woods to conduct laboratory research. And so the novel ends:

"This new quinine stuff may prove pretty good. We'll plug along on it for two or three years, and maybe we'll get something permanent—and probably we'll fail!"

The novelty of the work lies in the fact that the restlessness of the hero—in the novels with happy idyllic endings the idyllic seeker of freedom and adventure—becomes the external form of his spiritual tragedy: the answer sought in vain from science and, through science, from all the forms of existence. For every place he goes Martin Arrowsmith is looking for something, looking for himself, for peace, for happiness, for an answer which he can stand; but nothing ever satisfies him, except perhaps at one time the stupefactions of alcohol and his present stupefactions from fatigue in the laboratory. Everywhere he is tracked down and persecuted by an intolerable environment, which is now grotesque and vulgar (Pickerbaugh, the director in Nautilus), now empty and pretentious (Holabird in New York), now charlatan and self-seeking (Angus Duer in Chicago). Of the people in Martin's life who merit a little confidence, Max Gottlieb, the austere scientist who educates him to hard work, ends insane and abandoned; Gustaf Sondelius, the voluble and warmhearted lecturer, a great drinker and an even better friend of science and life, dies of plague at St. Hubert; and Leora, the perfect companion, a more serious and affectionate Alverna, the loyal comforter who even sacrifices herself for her defeated husband, and who is at the same time a hearty and happy daughter of the Midland, comes to the same end as Sondelius. Leora is a wonderful figure, the most beautiful flower (blooming in the somber atmosphere of *Arrowsmith*) of that whole springtime of eager young men and women in the early novels, the perfect poetic expression of that world of almost pagan freedom which, side by side with the sorrowful Babbitts, the spiritual torments, the controversy, Sinclair Lewis discovered in his native land.

This paganism returns and comes to an end in *Elmer Gantry*. The book's argument is apparently that many contemporary clergymen are frauds, while the rest are either fools or unhappy wretches forced by conscience to disavow what they can no longer believe. The argument has its merits, but the life of the book is something else again. The character of Elmer Gantry, seducer, sinner in all sorts, informer, liar, ignoramus, cheat, is delightfully sympathetic.

The book begins with a drinking bout and ends with a victory. For the whole time Gantry has been running around the United States, from theology student to commercial traveler, from commercial traveler to Methodist preacher in Europe, always vulgar, always "slangy" and "backslapping," always earthy, always a scoundrel. Gantry models his sermons on the speeches of Ingersoll,[5] and causes one of his seminary professors, who doubts certain dogmas, to be dismissed from the school and to die of want; Gantry meets his mistress in the sacristy, and promotes a crusade against vice in Zenith; Gantry lies, Gantry cheats, Gantry betrays, and still Gantry retains his care of souls and is a model of virtue in the States. I don't know whether Sinclair Lewis intended to make Gantry repulsive; certainly the intensity of the attack lends weight to the

5. Robert G. Ingersoll, atheistic and rhetorical orator of the last century; famous for his debate on the mortality of the soul, held in 1890 with Walt Whitman.

supposition; and, as a result, Lewis might well have relapsed to the level of *Main Street,* but his Middle Western nature saved him. However Lewis persists in piling on the head of Elmer Gantry all the vices and all the hypocrisies of the trade, the effect is only to give him a new power. The character is too robust and carnal and pagan, too unconsciously sincere and at peace with himself, too well adjusted, too entrepreneurial, this born leader of mobs, this spellbinder, this creator of grand enterprises.

He is ignorant, but he knows how to carry away an audience with words. He is vulgar and brutal, but he knows how to conquer all the women he likes. He is a sinner, but he restores power to his church. Before the eyes of Frank Shallard, the conscientious and ineffectual friend who is going to end badly among the victims, he fascinates congregations, builds a church, wards off blackmail, and ends triumphantly thanking his God.

Elmer Gantry has a grandiose mind. The scheme which strikes him like lightning on the bridge of the ship which is carrying him to Europe is not grotesque but exalting. Listen to him:

> He was walking the deck—but only in the body, for his soul was soaring among the stars—he was walking the deck alone, late at night, clenching his fists and wanting to shout as he saw it all clearly.
>
> He would combine in one association all the moral organizations in America—perhaps, later, in the entire world. He would be the executive of that combination; he would be the super-president of the United States, and some day the dictator of the world.
>
> Combine them all. . . .
>
> And the head of this united organization would be the Warwick of America, the man behind the throne . . . and that man, perhaps the most powerful man since the beginning of history, was going to be Elmer Gantry. Not even Napoleon or Alexander had been able to dictate what a whole nation should wear and eat and say and think. That, Elmer Gantry was about to do.

This character that in its supreme carnality has something of Victor Hugo's *Satyre* is, at bottom, and closely considered, nothing but a sublimation of the gross material type represented by Eddie Schwirtz (*The Job*). There converge in him, organized by art, the adventurous spirits of the young Middlewesterners, the earthy spirits of the hearty speakers of slang scattered through all the novels, and the generous nature of a person like Gustaf Sondelius. It is no offense to the author to declare that Elmer Gantry is, imaginatively speaking, quite autobiographical.

And as Gantry is the sublimation, almost the exasperation, of the crude and sensual type, long-standing with Lewis, so his companion—but not forever—Sharon Falconer, is the exasperation of the tormented, extravagant woman (Istra Nash) and of the affectionate and loyal friend (Leora). Sharon is an evangelical prophetess who goes on tour with a company of musicians and assorted helpers, and who every so often stops to preach, sing hymns, and save souls. She does not do these things from conviction. She is a hysteric, a mystic: she compares herself with Astarte, Frigga, and Hera. Her method is to conduct a mass meeting into which she imparts so much pathos that the listeners are thrown to the ground shouting that they are saved. An attendant counts the number of these converts and the lady then prints it in the newspapers. But not even Sharon is ludicrous. She is so extreme a type—as Gantry is, but she more than Gantry—that such ridicule as there is descends upon the paying public. She is admirable and, coldly viewed, she is, like Gantry, an organizer. In her fragility, then, this woman is also more tragic, since she doubts herself and abandons herself to Elmer like a fool, like a child. And she has a sense of the grandiose that surpasses even that of her lover. The great scene of her death, in the burning of a theater erected on an Atlantic beach for an evangelical meeting, under the great beaconlike cross that shines so far, has a solemn and genuine force, beyond rhetoric, of which, in quite a lot of literature, I do not know the equal.

Naturally, even this last-named novel has a mass of flaws. They derive from the theme. This way of insisting on types, and on questions of religious milieu, as described, is awkward for art, even when done with the usual facility, and with the continuous, by now organic, irony of style. But then, who can say if Lewis does *not* owe precisely the richness of the characters he has created to the various directions which the various programmatic intentions have given to his spirit?

However, the habit of depicting a type representative of a class does not cease with Elmer Gantry. The two novels that follow persist in the habit and suffer a little from it. But *The Man Who Knew Coolidge* (1928) has nothing to lose, it was already destroyed by another defect. The fact that nobody talks but Schmaltz—the entire book is a series of speeches which the hero delivers on the train, at home, to his friends, and before his club at the Congregational church—reduces the work to a pamphlet, a grotesque attack, in which a huge satiric mask holds the stage and nothing is discovered of his actions or of his life, except perhaps a glimpse or two of a trip to New York and to California. This is an unsuccessful book as, indeed, everybody has said.[6] As for its spirit, Schmaltz is a Babbitt drained of all his quiet rebelliousness, a Schwirtz drained even of his almost sympathetic, carefree, earthy materialism. This book that could not be a tragedy is an inept grotesque.

Dodsworth (1929) is more interesting, the story of an extremely rich industrialist from the customary Zenith who, as he begins to feel his age, discovers the emptiness of business and, half reluctant and half naive, accompanies his wife to Europe, where she inconsiderately neglects him; he, who no longer has anything to do, sadly spends his time suffering from his superfluity, humanly, like every Babbitt. Raymond Henry

6. Henry L. Stuart, "Mr. Lewis Goes Back to Babbitt," *New York Times Book Review,* 8 April 1928. This review understands the book (*The Man Who Knew Coolidge*) well, but has the defect of stubbornly referring the failure of the work to the close relationship of Schmaltz with Babbitt rather than to somewhat more serious reasons of construction.

has seen all this in *Dodsworth,*[7] and from it he concludes that this time Sinclair Lewis, the powerful creator, has mistaken himself. But is this the whole novel? All the Dodsworths' conversations with Europeans and with Americans, which Henry condemns as theoretical discussions of the relations between America and Europe, which presumably have nothing to do with the novel, are they really as useless and extraneous to the story as he appears to think? It seems to me that the story is quite different. Granted, there is the conjugal drama, granted, also, that some conversations recognizably result from the historical moment, and have no interest now; but isn't Sam Dodsworth's marital suffering in a way the visible form of another drama, more profound, exactly the one that Henry regrets Lewis left untouched? In short, don't we have in this novel the story of a melancholy American who, isolated and lost when away from his automobiles, finds himself face to face with a new world, Europe, which at first rejects him, irreconcilably (" 'We are culture and tradition, you are business and opportunists' ") , but little by little, in the end, permits him to understand it ("not a picturesque show but a normal and eager life") ? And not only this—which would still be nothing —but it is revealed to Sam Dodsworth, who no longer knew where to ground himself, disheartened by everything in his native land, how even the most serious traditions and realities of Europe are no greater than the labor that is being accomplished in America, and how he, an anonymous worker of the United States, is comparable to the anonymous European builders of cathedrals, *the* glory (to American eyes) of our tradition. Let him speak for himself:

Or possibly an artist? He had created something! He had no pictures in the academies, no books to be bound in levant, no arias nor flimsy furniture named after him, but every one of the twenty million motors on the roads of America had

7. Raymond Henry, "Un nouveau livre de Sinclair Lewis," *L'Européen,* 18 June 1930.

been influenced by his vision, a quarter of a century ago, of long, clean streamlines!

This is the true ordeal and the true catharsis of Dodsworth, crushed, from one side, by his gross American friends, and, from the other, by his wife, a useless and empty Europe fancier. It is a subtle bit of technique that lets Sam make his spiritual discoveries in the solitude and anguish to which his wife abandons him. Until the triumphant discovery and liberation of the concluding chapters: an American, Edith Cortright, who knows how to live in Venice like an old patrician and in Naples like a Neapolitan, or even like a peasant, and who, like Dodsworth, has understood Europe and lives it, seeking from it the land and simplicity, the real and essential things, also believes in him and loves him.

And this book has another novelty in reserve: once again it is a book with a happy ending. The final ironic sentence, which Henry likes so much, seems to me not only useless but discordant. The conclusion is Sam's happiness. It is a meditative idyll, wherein we see Sinclair Lewis, after novels of no confidence and melancholy laughter, return, rich with experiences and liberated from naiveté, to the characters of his youth, hopeful about America. Does this change foreshadow a new creative cycle?

Taken as a whole, one thing is especially conspicuous in these novels by Lewis. The characters, and with them the author, are great provincial types. In every sense of the word, great. They begin as innocents. Those from the prairies go to be provincials in New York and those from New York go to be provincials in Europe. They end in dignity, but—charlatans or distinguished scientists or industrialists as they are—a room full of people in evening dress will always make them uneasy.

Still, it was such people—with whom the Middle West, the American heartland, perpetuates itself in art—that the national literature needed. It would carry me too far afield to tell how and with which writers this character was born. But, certainly, without its provincials a literature has no nerve. And the provincials and farmers include not only carefree Milt Daggett, full-blooded Elmer Gantry, and thoughtful Martin Arrowsmith, but the least expected types, like Sharon, who, before exercising control over crowds and playing the role of Cleopatra, was a stenographer at Utica (U.S.A.), and who has in her so much human energy that, out of the still hesitant Elmer Gantry from Paris, Kansas, she is able to make for a moment an impassioned and genuine lover and—without irony—a grandiose charlatan forever. Even the sad and right-minded Babbitt participates in this quality of the safe and sane province and, after all, even he, like Dodsworth, is a laborious creator of the race of people who have contributed to the richness of America. And Zenith, the ridiculous city, enlarged, is only the bustling village of the Midland, to which America—and even Sam lets us know it—owes so much.

The true provincial nature of Sinclair Lewis is shown in the use of slang and the vernacular. This kind of jargon and dialect, the national expression of America, is understood by him, loved, and finally made into poetry, resulting in the true creation of a language—the American vernacular: a thing of which there has been no example since the times when the neo-Latin peoples stabilized their virgin idioms in works of art and life. Before Lewis, American slang was local color or journalistic improvisation. Perhaps only O. Henry, that happy mad genius, used it in such a way as to compose a literary language. But in the others—Mark Twain, William Dean Howells, the greatest writers—the American vernacular is still too much in the condition of the Negro in the speeches of Jupiter ("The Gold Bug" of Edgar Poe): local color. In the authoritative works of H. L. Mencken,[8] one sees better than anywhere else

8. Mencken, p. 270. Mencken isn't talking only about Lewis in this examination of the new language: he mentions Ring W. Lardner of Chicago, writer of "baseball" stories, Caroline Lockhart and John V. A. Weaver and Carl Sandburg, poets, but surely, above all

the debt America owes Sinclair Lewis for this achievement, and Mencken was writing only at the time of *Main Street,* in 1920.

The ultimate foundation, therefore, of the poetry of Sinclair Lewis, seems to me this powerful and happy world, this earthy spirit. Behind ironies and subtleties, behind problems and culture, our author has always remained the restless and versatile young man from Sauk Center, Minnesota, who does not understand music, who does not understand (he says so himself) paintings, but who has dabbled in all the trades and who loves to tell his companions tales of his experiences—exuberant stories, even when tragic, stories of the region—where, in every one of them, there persists something of his people's open and healthy sense of life.

---

these, among whom several have the air of being specialists or dilettantes—the same thing, in this case—rises Sinclair Lewis, who, with the importance of certain of his works, with the amplitude and assurance of his means, has definitively consecrated the American language as distinct from English, and as literary. I don't speak, naturally, of the new generation—the writers who began after the war—because these, beyond argument, write in the new language.

SHERWOOD ANDERSON

It is difficult to talk in Italy about American writers precisely because the greatest of them have had to solve in their work problems of a historical nature about which almost none of our public has any idea. And it is not only difficult to *talk about* these writers, but even to read them with understanding, for although it is all very well to say that a work of art is such insofar as it escapes the historical circumstances that produced it and creates an imaginative world of its own, etc., these are mere words. In fact, the work of art moves us and allows us to comprehend it only as long as it retains historical interest for us, answers to some problem of ours, answers, in short, our need for practical life. There is no such thing as art for art's sake. Even the most irresponsibly Parnassian lyric will solve for the reader—it would have to be a somewhat old-fashioned reader, to be sure—a practical problem: how to live in a dream.

Now to understand the modern American novelists—I allude to the group, more famous than known, of the three innovators, Theodore Dreiser, Sinclair Lewis, and Sherwood Anderson—it is not only necessary to recognize the common historical need their works met, but it is indispensable, unless you want to waste your breath, to find an image, a historical parallel, through which you can relate to familiar conditions at home those transatlantic acts of life that the majority of readers are rather pleased to regard as so exotic.

And the parallel exists, clear and exact. We might think of the significance, for Italian literature, of the discovery of regions, which went hand in hand with the quest for national unity, a discovery that belongs to the last part of the eighteenth and to the entire nineteenth century. From Alfieri on down, all the Italian writers try, sometimes and indeed often unconsciously, to achieve a more profound national unity through penetrating always further the character of their own region, as it exists in them, their *true* nature, thus to achieve the creation of a human awareness and a language rich with all the blood of the province and with all the dignity of life renewed. And especially my countrymen from Piedmont might think about these things, for it is in Piedmont that the urgency of this aspiration is still felt most powerfully and is furthest from realization, lost as we now are behind too much specialization of dialect. Let us, Piedmontese, think of it, for it was in our name, with Alfieri, that this renaissance historically commenced; and yet, from Alfieri himself, and then through D'Azeglio, Abba, to Calandra, or even later, we have never had that man and that work which, in addition to being most dear to us, would truly achieve that universality and originality which would make him comprehensible to all men and not only to his countrymen. This is our still unsatisfied need. Meanwhile, the American novelists of whom I speak have in fact met the corresponding need of their nation and region. We must, therefore, learn from them.

And so the intelligent reader, when he hears about Ohio, Illinois, Michigan, Minnesota, Iowa, Indiana, Dakota, Nebraska, should leave behind (after having enjoyed the rich harmony of the Indian names) all exoticism, and instead imagine in our colors those places that, eighty or so years ago, were prairies and forests which a first Anglo-Saxon generation was laboriously breaking, amid austerities and almost biblical exertions, and which the second and third generations were cultivating, with no less weariness and even some blasphemy, or were meanwhile losing to a proletariat, fecund and flooding from all the ports of Europe, Germans, Swedes, Bohemians, and Italians, who took away from the pioneers of the Middle West even the aura of the chosen people. At this point the novels of Dreiser and Lewis, and especially of Anderson, begin.

Huge plains gray with misery and labor, tiny communities full of gossip and narrow-mindedness, artisans who meet at the drugstore, a few of them already rich, the farmer; lots of wheat, lots of corn, lots of fruit. Cabbage soup and apple pie. But the Latins and the Slavs—the continental Europeans—have to plant the vine there, or, dropping the metaphor, their imagination. All the new writers are sons of this fusion. There are Swedes, Germans, Jews, Italians. That mixture of stocks which already in the middle of the century, in a New England Puritan and Quaker (Dutch and British) had put quicksilver in the veins of Walt Whitman and Herman Melville, at the end of the century repeats the miracle. The literature that discovers America is born again precisely of this escape into foreign blood. Sherwood Anderson will even state the problem of the national renaissance in terms of the fusion between Anglo-Saxons and Latins—or Negroes—in any case, people who know how to play and to sing.

But if these writers, who all began after 1900, had described their region only as it was until the 1880's, the Middle West would never have come alive, and they themselves would have been only the usual re-creators of the past, quite attractive ones even, but with no new life to teach us Piedmontese, who in this genre have our own great writers: Edoardo Calandra and Augusto Monti. In the 1880's, a cyclone passes through America. Large-scale industrialism is wed to the resources of the country, it absorbs all the national formulas of conquest and optimism, it opens up a practical field to what had until then been only mystical aspiration, it clears away and transforms all the ancient usages. The towns of the interior, with their gossipy and closed-minded inhabitants and with their modest names of Camden, Willow Springs, Gopher Prairie, Old Harbor, Sauk Center, Sandusky, become the smoky and noisy centers, active and optimistic, that the whole world knows: Cleveland, Springfield, Detroit, Akron, Pittsburgh, and, above all, gigantic, the metropolis, Chicago. The factories engulf everything. Craftsmen, once content with their little corners, their circumstances, become operatives who change their trade every day, indifferent to the job. The fields are worked by machine, and they too are great factories. A man becomes a hero because he invents a lever or a special connecting rod. The legend of the American businessman is created. Chicago welcomes them all. The new gods are painful grotesques. The king of petroleum is born, along with the king of steel, the king of canned meat, the king of wheat. In short, contemporary America begins.

From this world Lewis derived his marvelous provincial types, who seem so funny and are in fact so serious, the most profound and definitive products of that civilization, the vulgar and stern-souled peasants, loudmouthed and tormented in the great temporary cities. From this world Anderson, projecting in general terms the present contrast through the historical epoch when it began to show itself (the years of his youth), has drawn the saddest and most thoughtful and most decisive descriptions of modern life, at once elemental and extremely complicated, cerebral and unlearned, beautiful with a beauty which goes well beyond the printed page.

He touches upon a number of purely national issues in his books, and of these it is useless to speak now: it is enough if everyone bear in mind what is in his work the problem and the condition of life, which define and transcend all national issues. For Anderson, the whole modern world is a contrast between city and country, between sincerity and empty pretense, between nature and petty men. How much this idea touches us too, I think it needless to say. And by what margin we are inferior in vital power to young America we may see in the fact that a problem that gave America works such as those of which I speak gave us literary caricatures only, *stracittà* and *strapaese*.

Sherwood Anderson published his first book in 1916. At the age of fifty-five he is still writing. We can also imagine that he would have been scribbling a little earlier. There still remain at least thirty years of silence. These thirty years he spent wandering around, through the Middle West, from the Ohio village where he was born, to Chicago, to New Orleans, and to New York, in the cyclone of industrialism, as stableboy, worker, soldier, journalist, and businessman. And then, one day, he abandons business and secretary, fleeing, it has been said, like a monk in the desert, all alone and ready to write books. He publishes the first, and he has never quit.

Sherwood Anderson saw all of American life during the Theodore Roosevelt era. He plunged into it in youth, he lived it and he suffered it—he loved it—he sought in every way to escape it; and one day he discovered that, since the years of childhood—from the father, a feckless good-for-nothing, from the grandmother, a resolute Italian, soil and blood, drinker and centenarian—he had always been an escapist, a dreamer, a teller of tales. And then he decided to do nothing but tell tales for life, regretting only that he was not a poet in the oral tradition and expressing himself in this revealing definition of style: the writer's whole effort is the attempt to render the gestures and expressions of the narrator himself (in *Horses and Men*). Naturally, the stories he wrote are always the same story: the story of a person stifled by the atmosphere of Ohio (the region, the Middle West), by the atmosphere of the factories, by the atmosphere of Puritanism and of literature, and either it stops here—and then we have the melancholy and tragic stories of his early manner, up to 1923, the tales, in general of the desperate and resigned titles ("Nobody Knows," "Surrender," "Loneliness," "Death," "Sophistication," in *Winesburg, Ohio,* 1919; "Unlighted Lamps," "Out of Nowhere Into Nothing," in *The Triumph of the Egg,* 1921; and "Unused," in *Horses and Men,* 1923) ; or else he succeeds in making his escape from these things, and the flight is the imagination, inner freedom, sincerity, a pagan and poetic sensuality. On the whole these are the more autobiographical stories: the artist, the village daydreamer, the enemy of Chicago and New York salons. Some stories of *Horses and Men* already announce this vein, such as those about horses (the passion for beautiful flesh), or "An Ohio Pagan" (in which Christ becomes a Greek god while remaining a Middlewestern young man) ; there also appears the omnipresent figure of the craftsman in love with his craft.

But essentially this liberation is the substance of the more mature and comprehensive volumes: *A Story Teller's Story* (1924), "imaginative" autobiography of few facts and much inner life, entirely concerned to solve the problem of "this big, noisy, growing and groping America"; *Dark Laughter* (1925), of which I will speak later; *Tar* (1926), the fond recollection of his village childhood, but always with an eye on the artist being born there; and *Hello Towns!* (1929), the most curious and fantastic experience of a year spent publishing a rural weekly, where, in the humor of the incidents, in the good nature of the advice, and in the depth of the observation of contemporary America, there is definitely expressed that simple love which only Sherwood Anderson knows how to feel—in the midst of the most complicated labors, and with a miracle of popularization practically fourteenth-century—for the humble life, ordinary, sincere, of the great body of America. In the meantime, here and there since 1921, and then collected in 1927, there is the poetry of *A New Testament,* sober meditations on the need of imaginative expression which torments America and the author.

The most important novel by this man is still *Dark Laughter,* in what I have called the second manner, for it sums up within itself all the scattered themes of the other tales since 1916, some of which had been treated more clearly, more successfully elsewhere, but never so definitively. It is the story of a Chicago newspaperman who is bored and feels useless, telling little lies to the public and making the rounds of salons with his intellectual, fiction-writing wife. Sometimes he gets drunk with a colleague, but they only end up talking of impotence and degeneration. Finally, one day he throws over everything, changes his name, and lazily descends the Mississippi, by train and by boat, as far as New Orleans. Here he is imbued with the pleasures of indolence and of Negro laughter, of Negro song, and of the Negro spirit. Then he retraces his course and stops at Old Harbor, Indiana, where he had lived in childhood and where he finds a job—as a common laborer, varnishing automobile wheels in a bustling *American* factory—which leaves him utterly indifferent.

The narrative commences only at this point, but the gist of it is what I have summarized. For Bruce Dudley—the new name—is a complete Sherwood Anderson and he imagines, he meditates, he relives, *he recounts to himself,* indolently, from time to time, the tenuous bonds with the facts of Old Harbor, the past life. There stirs in his memory—to the rhythm of sentences meditative and languidly solemn—the great times of the River, when the true American life, the life of people who laughed and sang, moved on the Mississippi and the Negroes were Negroes and Mark Twain, not yet caged by Puritan ideas (by New England, the negation of America), from them created heroic fable with the books of Tom Sawyer and Huck Finn. Bruce Dudley (Sherwood Anderson) is, as I have said, a storyteller, and sees life only as a story which has to be told, and speaks so slowly and thoughtfully because everything he says is laboring within his mind, transforming itself into a tale. What might have been the writer's ruin turns into his poetry instead, since no one is further from literature and more *living* than he, no one more enamoured of things and of the world, in an almost sensual way. This man even gets to the point of saying that in order to be a writer it is *also* a good idea to read books.

At Old Harbor, Indiana, Bruce Dudley had spent his childhood. And it is this vein of the book that most echoes and recapitulates Anderson's earlier stories. The little gray village, which is stifling as a town (*Winesburg, Ohio*), and which makes us nostalgic when it becomes an *American* city (*Poor White,* 1920), is still, fortunately, the material of these pages. Bruce Dudley remembers the great days when the fields were fields and the River was the River and he sees those times mirrored in Sponge Martin, his friend on the job, an amusing old fellow who knows how to laugh and enjoy himself and who was once a good craftsman, while now he works as a painter in a factory, stunned and sodden. Together with his childhood there comes to Dudley's mind his mother, she who had already appeared in the autobiography as a taciturn and superior woman, from another people (the grandmother is Italian), noble in the midst of the most sordid affairs, the ideal (for Anderson) of that European world which he imagines as so close to the soil, so craftsmanlike, so much *the Mississippi of long ago.*

Meanwhile, the wife of the owner and boss of the factory—the hated industrialist, efficient and Puritan, who is underneath a child, a little man, even pathetic (Babbitt!)—the wife of the owner has her own fancies. And she too, stimulated by fleeting, casual encounters with Dudley, *tells to herself* her previous life. She recalls Europe where, after the war, she lived in charlatan and vicious artistic circles (the salons of Chicago!). As it happens, she heard a horrified lady (and this one was no virgin) describe the sexual orgies that took place at a party after the end of the war, and all the memories of the war are the same, extremely bitter, shock waves from the useless slaughter and the odious rhetoric. Her traveling companion (female) tries to seduce her. All together, this world disgusts the young lady who, in order to escape it, marries Fred, the future industrialist, who is also disgusted with Europe. They return. And then—America is mean—the interior flight, Madame Bovary. But it is no longer false education that leads the lady into errors; it is the most serious enigma of holy nature, which created the loveliest stories in *The Triumph of the Egg,* and which reappears and is now the same thing as the imaginative liberation of the man. And the landscape that accompanies the erotic dreams is, as in the stories of 1921, the best landscape—elemental and genuine and total—in nature, the Mississippi.

The conclusion is that Bruce Dudley is hired as a gardener at the Grey house and subsequently runs away with the wife. At this point, that universality of Anderson's, of which I spoke —not city, not country, but the virginity of the land working itself out into our urban contemporary life (something, in a serious vein, like the grotesque talking cartoons of that other dizzy American, the creator of Mickey Mouse)—Anderson's universality achieves a tone that if it were not what it is (the perfect fusion of the two kinds) you might call it primitive. These pages—the instinctive rapprochement in spring, and the flight, together with the impotent reactions of Fred, wholly content to take part in a parade for the inauguration of a statue to the Fallen, and entirely disposed, humanly, pitifully, not to notice that the other couple want to run away, and who then laughs, laughs desperately, with a sense of relief, as "in a battle, when one is wounded"—are among the most immediate and profound things of contemporary America.

With respect to Anderson, it is important to discredit the legend that this already classic and exceedingly personal writer is a Joycean. In *Dark Laughter* Anderson mentions Joyce and tells us that he liked *Ulysses* enormously. And certainly his own way of alluding to ideas as parallel to external facts might well fool the reader. Now it is readily understandable how Joyce might interest Anderson—Anderson who, in America, is an innovator against the conventional Puritan and Victorian literary mode, which is all-powerful there, or used to be. But we should not forget that he is also interested, and perhaps more so, through a simplicity of spirit and culture which we have destroyed to our great loss, in the Russian novelists and the French naturalists. For Anderson the supreme ideal is the story; we have seen his techniques in the definition of style which I cited. And in *Hello Towns!* Anderson parenthetically informs us that Joyce doesn't know how to tell a story. It is a complication that the novelty of Joyce, like Freudian ideas, finds a weak spot in America on account of Puritan prejudice, with the result that the enemies of Puritanism feel themselves obliged to collect with gusto every European book that treats sex frankly, while we, in general, associate sexual problems with Boccaccio or Rabelais.

It remains a fact that between the sexual pages of James Joyce (tedious gray swamps of notations and notations, where every so often some feature is barely visible, but for itself, for its singularity, not for its contribution to the construction of a character, and independently of all the mechanical apparatus of the new method) and the pages of tranquil narrative in "The New Englander," in *The Triumph of the Egg,* for example, which describes the obsession of a girl from a Puritan family who, having emigrated to the West, feels irrepressible instincts awakening in her and forcing her to lose herself and to blend herself with the stormy inebriating breath of the wheat fields, there is no possible comparison.

Another reason why Sherwood Anderson likes, or at least takes an interest in, James Joyce and Joyceanism and the work —to me, unbearable—of Madame Gertrude Stein, is that in that abundance and freedom and joy of words existing by themselves, or almost (vicious in Europeans), the American, the *Middle Westerner,* finds a substitute for the centuries of tradition which are lacking to give flavor to his language, to furnish *earthiness* to the living material of his tales, such as the Indians had given to their words, tying them to places:

Once the Indians danced there, made feasts there. They threw poems about like seeds on a wind. Names of rivers, names of towns. Ohio! Illinois! Keokuk! Chicago! Illinois! Michigan!

It is that problem of the soil, through which we Europeans, according to Anderson, enjoy our existence more because through the ages we are more tied to our material. And here you think of Walt Whitman, who likewise was crazy about Indian names, who made long lists of words with the intention of restoring their virgin purity, and who defended the new vernacular of the States.

Anderson's style! Not a crude dialect still too local—like that of our dialect specialists who, even in the most distinguished instances, still retain something a little petty—but a new texture of English, entirely constructed of American idioms, a style no longer *dialect* but *language,* reworked in the mind, re-created, *poetry.* In a tale written by Anderson there is always heard an American speaker, *the living man.* I have already said how he feels this tale sanely and vitally, and may conclude by once more recalling the pages of *A Story Teller's Story,* where he conjures up the bizarre figure of his father, a dionysiac loafer who only knows how to invent stories—in every sense stories—and who tells them to the rural people of Ohio, of the West, to provincial families, as a bard, as a trouvère (consequently Sherwood Anderson has very little literature in his bones, and we can impose it on him without fear, for he is always genuine), as a trouvère, I was saying, but gay, free and easy, craftsmanlike, obtaining in exchange for the stories wine, a lodging for the night, and affection.

And, to end with, what better than a page from *Dark Laughter,* in which, to express that sensual but healthy passion (of which I spoke) for words and poetry, the Negroes sing, the Negroes with their "red tongues":

From the throats of the ragged black men as they trotted up and down the landing-stage, strange haunting notes. Words were caught up, tossed about, held in the throat. Word-lovers, sound-lovers. . . . Unconscious love of inanimate things lost to the whites—skies, the river, a moving boat—black mysticism —never expressed except in song or in the movements of bodies. The bodies of the black workers belonged to each other as the sky belonged to the river. Far off now, down river, where the sky was splashed with red, it touched the face of the river. The tones from the throats of the black workers touched each other, caressed each other. . . .

The words coming from the throats of the black workers could not be understood by the boy but were strong and lovely. . . . Streaming reds, browns, golden yellows coming out of black throats. . . . Sounds caught and held in black throats. . . . The word, as meaning, of no importance. Perhaps words were always unimportant. There were strange words about a "banjo dog." What was a "banjo dog"? "Ah, my banjo dog! Oh, oh! Oh, oh! Ah, my banjo dog!"

THE SPOON RIVER ANTHOLOGY

The few references so far made in Europe to this book reveal the false attitude that, toward everything American, we are pleased to take. Even Régis Michaud, who, as far as I know, is *the* person in all the world who has up to now best estimated that literature, having arrived in his *Panorama*[1] at the paragraph "Edgar Lee Masters" (p. 188), implies that *Spoon River Anthology* is essentially a work representative of the encaged and leveled throngs who are outcasts from Puritanism and from the new civilization of the United States. Better not to notice, then (for we would thus give them an importance they don't deserve), what certain Italian journalists from America say of the book. They have reduced *Spoon River* to an ethnic cultural document, a journalistic mirror of a civilization that, as they present it to us, ought really to begin to nauseate us, by contrast with (and so they clip the wings of American civilization) "our two-thousand-year tradition." When two boys quarrel, it is certain that, coming short of reasons, the competition begins. "I'm the marshal's son." "And I'm the captain's."

Everyone knows how to say that the great merit of Lee Mas-

1. Régis Michaud, *Littérature américaine* (Paris: Kra, 1928).

ters is to have begun, in his country, the realistic, merciless description of provincial people, villagers, Puritans. The dates speak for themselves: *Spoon River,* 1915; *Winesburg, Ohio,* 1919; *My Antonía* [1918] and *Main Street,* 1920. So Edgar Lee Masters holds the record. He is the father of contemporary literature. After which, we can go on to talk about other things. Now, leaving aside the fact that in America the village had passed through Hawthorne's crucible at least as early as 1846, it would seem to me a rather feeble title for the new writers, that of having for all originality called attention to their local environment, full of local problems, and then of having solved these problems in terms of local life. If we want to read about provincial life, there are already too many European writers who have dealt with it.

Where, then, *is* the interest of these books? The truth seems to me in the first place this: to take Edgar Lee Masters for an anti-Puritan, as so many wish to do, is to reduce him to a rather feeble muckraker. Problems of this sort are already boring enough in your own house. It is true that, as in all books, American or European, worth anything at all, there is in *Spoon River* an indigenous environment and experience, an appeal to ways of life and national types that will strike the eye of every modest moviegoer as old acquaintances. But this is only the book's honesty, its direct inspiration by life, its matter, and, as I said, all books of any merit more or less display this characteristic.

We must understand that, given this national background, the important achievement lies not in the assault on certain Puritan customs—an assault that in any case amounts to very little in the book—but in the really Puritanical energy with which, going well beyond the historical moment, the book confronts the problem of the meaning of existence and the problems of one's own behavior: the energy and the problems are essentially moral and of an almost biblical tone. If in the exploration some blow is struck at the Puritanical historical structure of the country, this may be very interesting to the

Americans, who themselves observe this structure all around them and on top of them, but it means little to us, except insofar as the writer's genius has transformed what for the natives and the scholars is an obvious reference into a metaphor which is no longer a mere historical name but a new creation. And in order to do this, to succeed in this work of creation—which I think Masters in large part realized—it seems to me all too obvious to say that the writer had to love his environment, to take pleasure in his own characters, to feel them born in his spirit.

The animus of destructive caricature is extremely rare in Lee Masters. The passion of every one of the hundreds of souls buried at Spoon River becomes his passion, and quite literally the poet speaks to us through the mouth of every one. This ever-renewed exploration of the worth of existence *in articulo mortis* possesses such seriousness and candor that, even in the case of Lee Masters, we have to fall back on what is by now a commonplace in the history of American culture: in the fight against Puritanism are always found the greatest Puritans.

Spoon River Anthology, published piece by piece in a Middle Western weekly,[2] is a large collection of graveyard epitaphs, placed on the lips—according to good classical convention—of the dead themselves, from a typical American small town, Spoon River. Naturally one immediately thinks that here is an influence of the *Antologia Palatina.* And, apart from the spirit which, in those Hellenistic farewells to life, by virgins, sailors, courtesans, warriors, philosophers, farmers, and poets, is a fond or stoic regret for the light of the sun—while we shall see all the modern complexity and transcendence of the aspirations of Spoon River—apart from the spirit, it is not impossible that Lee Masters drew from those epigrams the formal idea of his book: the title and the shape of the epi-

2. *Reedy's Mirror.* In 1915 it was collected in volume form and published by Macmillan. In 1916 there was a new edition with new poems.

taph, swift, sententious, classical. But even in this respect we have a renewal: the form, although preserving the lines of verse, disregards rhyme and meter. This has begun to bother many people: they have found that in this way an odiously prosaic style emerges. It is useless to argue the matter; if one does not himself feel the tragic and definitive solemnity of those sparse phrases, placed at the end of a life, in a versification so sober and quiet that it simply has the function of indicating the thought, I doubt if any lecture can ever educate him.

Take, for example, this epitaph:

FRANCIS TURNER

I could not run or play
In boyhood.
In manhood I could only sip the cup,
Not drink—
For scarlet-fever left my heart diseased.
Yet I lie here
Soothed by a secret none but Mary knows:
There is a garden of acacia,
Catalpa trees, and arbors sweet with vines—
There on that afternoon in June
By Mary's side—
Kissing her with my soul upon my lips
It suddenly took flight.

Here the pauses are not arbitrary. The first ones hammer precisely because they express the recurrent mockery of that fate. And when, as in the fifth line, a thought has no reason to be broken, the writer makes no bones about writing it out to its full length. We must further observe the importance of the brief pause after "By Mary's side," which makes us hold our breath before the flight that follows.

Taking up again, instead, the other charge, much more serious, which is lately used to attack America under the form of praise, the Spoon River dead are supposed to be the outcasts of that civilization, who argue against it by revealing their secret wounds. Here our journalists immediately attack: a humanity of the insane asylum, look what America offers us! But our two thousand years . . . See if this man seems to you an outcast:

BLIND JACK

I had fiddled all day at the county fair.
But driving home "Butch" Weldy and Jack McGuire,
Who were roaring full, made me fiddle and fiddle
To the song of *Susie Skinner,* while whipping the horses
Till they ran away.
Blind as I was, I tried to get out
As the carriage fell in the ditch,
And was caught in the wheels and killed.
There's a blind man here with a brow
As big and white as a cloud.
And all we fiddlers, from highest to lowest,
Writers of music and tellers of stories,
Sit at his feet,
And hear him sing of the fall of Troy.

But naturally this is chosen from a great mass of possible examples. A book which begins with an elegy on the cemetery, and continues with unhappy husbands, adulterous wives, cantankerous bachelors, babies born dead, and where practically everyone laments the fact that he missed out in life, might well seem, in a casual reading, a collection of clinical cases. The difference is only in the way the poet looks at his dead, not with morbid or polemical satisfaction, not with that pseudoscientific lack of sensibility which is now unfortunately so popular in the States, but with an awareness at once strict and sympathetic toward the griefs of all, the vanities of all; from all he elicits a confession, from all he extorts definitive answers, not to derive therefrom a scientific or sociological document, but only out of passion for human truth. That life is a cemetery of frustrated ambitions, of reality to be suffered, of "clipped wings," there is no need for psychoanalysis to discover: Solomon already knew as much. In short, I mean that although some characters of the *Anthology* may seem stunted, stifled by a particular environment, that is not quite the spirit of the book; on the contrary, it contemplates and shares—evaluating them with its powerful objectivity—the countless defeats, endeavors, battles, and rare victories of life against death, of spirit against chaos, of which this provincial village which is also the world is the battleground. Needless to say, there are no symbols. Everything is vigorously alive, realized, present; in a word, everything is poetry.

The importance of this book lies in the answer never definitively given, but forever renewed through each person, the conviction, sorrowfully felt on every page, that however satisfactory and final any solution of life may seem, there will always be other people who remain outside it. Neither optimism nor pessimism is the answer, which rather depends on a spirit of inquiry continuously renewed. Like the dead souls in Dante, who are more alive than in life, the dead of Spoon River prolong in sepulchral form all their frustrations and their passions. But here the parallel ends, since Dante's dead have a universal system in which they are included, and none of the damned dreams of criticizing his lot, while those of Spoon River, even though dead, have found no answers, least of all those who say they have. This book of poems is quintessentially modern, in its spirit of inquiry, in the inadequacy of every formula, in its need at once individual and social. You find that a child's lament, dead of tetanus while playing, rises to the same cosmic importance as the ecstacy of a scholar who spent his life in adoration of heaven and earth. In an epilogue, there is a sort of Faustian miracle play, where the character of the devil who continues to create wretched lives, to foment quarrels, and to toy with his creatures, is opposed by the spectacle of life triumphant, of harmonious laws, a kind of Shelleyan hymn to the liberated world, and which concludes:

> Infinite Law,
> Infinite Life.

But this hardly concerns the voices of Spoon River. The problem of each of those dead souls remains forever the same, frozen on the stone of his graveyard testament.

To make choices among these epitaphs is a little like sacrilege. As always in these cases, the ideal thing would be to have a publisher willing to publish a translation of the entire book. But they fear it wouldn't sell. Therefore, let's look at a few selected passages. So inclusive is its experience, I think everyone can find in this book his own epitaph. The collection ranges from an unborn fetus to a converted philosopher. Here is the first:

A stalk of the earth-sphere,
Frail as star-light;
Waiting to be drawn once again
Into creation's stream.
But next time to be given birth
Gazed at by Raphael and St. Francis
Sometimes as they pass.
For I am their little brother,
To be known clearly face to face
Through a cycle of birth hereafter run.
You may know the seed and the soil;
You may feel the cold rain fall,
But only the earth-sphere, only heaven
Knows the secret of the seed
In the nuptial chamber under the soil.
Throw me into the stream again,
Give me another trial—
Save me, Shelley!

Or again, a child dead with its mother:

Dust of my dust,
And dust with my dust,
O, child who died as you entered the world,
Dead with my death!
Not knowing Breath, though you tried so hard,
With a heart that beat when you lived with me,
And stopped when you left me for Life.
It is well, my child. For you never traveled
The long, long way that begins with school days,
When little fingers blur under the tears
That fall on the crooked letters.
And the earliest wound, when a little mate
Leaves you alone for another;

And sickness, and the face of Fear by the bed;
The death of a father or mother;
Or shame for them, or poverty;
The maiden sorrow of school days ended;
And eyeless Nature that makes you drink
From the cup of Love, though you know it's poisoned;
To whom would your flower-face have been lifted?
Botanist, weakling? Cry of what blood to yours?—
Pure or foul, for it makes no matter,
It's blood that calls to our blood.
And then your children—oh, what might they be?
And what your sorrow? Child! Child!
Death is better than Life!

And here is the philosopher:

THE VILLAGE ATHEIST

Ye young debaters over the doctrine
Of the soul's immortality,
I who lie here was the village atheist,
Talkative, contentious, versed in the arguments
Of the infidels.
But through a long sickness
Coughing myself to death
I read the *Upanishads* and the poetry of Jesus.
And they lighted a torch of hope and intuition
And desire which the Shadow,
Leading me swiftly through the caverns of darkness,
Could not extinguish.
Listen to me, ye who live in the senses
And think through the senses only:
Immortality is not a gift,
Immortality is an achievement;
And only those who strive mightily
Shall possess it.

This way of treating a life lyrically, of talking about it almost in the abstract, giving its atmosphere, so to speak, and not the facts, is often found in the *Anthology* and is very dangerous. The irrepressibly Puritan nature of the author—that is to say, his clerical moralizing—sometimes makes an epitaph into a cloudy, abstract purple patch, an echo from his innumerable other works where the resounding and ceaseless lyrical torrent comes down all veiled in vapor.[3] But in this book, the need of brevity, of emphasis, and of definition of the characters only rarely permits Lee Masters to blunder.

He obtains effectiveness, and also greater originality, by more directly condensing a life into an episode magnified to total significance, or into a series of powerful actions, the barely outlined muscular system of an existence. Sometimes the episode has a slight ironic or polemic tone and proves nothing more than the author's felicity in striking out eternal lines on the material order of a gossip, simply by virtue of his *sub specie aeternitatis* judgment.

A. D. BLOOD

If you in the village think that my work was a good one,
Who closed the saloons and stopped all playing at cards,
And haled old Daisy Fraser [4] before Justice Arnett,
In many a crusade to purge the people of sin;
Why do you let the milliner's daughter Dora,
And the worthless son of Benjamin Pantier
Nightly make my grave their unholy pillow?

This Dora is met again entire in the story of her whole life.

DORA WILLIAMS

When Reuben Pantier ran away and threw me
I went to Springfield. There I met a lush,
Whose father just deceased left him a fortune.
He married me when drunk. My life was wretched.
A year passed and one day they found him dead.
That made me rich. I moved on to Chicago.
After a time met Tyler Rountree, villain.
I moved on to New York. A gray-haired magnate
Went mad about me—so another fortune.
He died one night right in my arms, you know.
(I saw his purple face for years thereafter.)
There was almost a scandal. I moved on,
This time to Paris. I was now a woman,
Insidious, subtle, versed in the world and rich.
My sweet apartment near the Champs Élysées
Became a center for all sorts of people,

3. I allude especially to *Lee* (1926) and to *Domesday Book* (1920).
4. The village prostitute.

Musicians, poets, dandies, artists, nobles,
Where we spoke French and German, Italian, English.
I wed Count Navigato, native of Genoa.
We went to Rome. He poisoned me, I think.
Now in the Campo Santo overlooking
The sea where young Columbus dreamed new worlds,
See what they chiseled: "*Contessa Navigato*
Implora eterna quiete." [5]

The tragedy which issues here from a great mass of experiences, organized biographically, elsewhere emerges from a contrast, from a terrible irony at the end of life, from one of those jokes that delight the devil of the epilogue. Speaking of the devil, it would be well to rule out any derivation of the *Anthology* from the *Mémoires du Diable* by Frédéric Soulié. Soulié's is a great and original book, but I must say that all those subtle and dramatic analyses of high and low French society during the Restoration, those diabolical X-rays of a humanity lost in blind passions, or in passions that have been reduced to blindness, have little to do with the desperate tensions of the souls of Spoon River, for whom all of life is concluded in a brief memory and whose pathos is born of the contrast between this brevity and the immensity of their aspirations. Not to mention the devil himself, who in the *Anthology* appears only in an epilogue independent of the work, while in the *Mémoires* he enters with supernatural machinery to break up the great commedia into a series of episodes. Anyhow, returning to our subject, here is one of those ironies of existence, the case of the impresario of *pompes funèbres:*

JEDUTHAN HAWLEY

There would be a knock at the door
And I would arise at midnight and go to the shop,
Where belated travelers would hear me hammering
Sepulchral boards and tacking satin.
And often I wondered who would go with me
To the distant land, our names the theme
For talk, in the same week, for I've observed

5. In Italian in the text.

Two always go together.
Chase Henry was paired with Edith Conant;
And Jonathan Somers with Willie Metcalf;
And Editor Hamblin with Francis Turner,
When he prayed to live longer than Editor Whedon . . .
And I, the solemnest man in town,
Stepped off with Daisy Fraser.

Or this other one:

WALTER SIMMONS

My parents thought that I would be
As great as Edison or greater:
For as a boy I made balloons
And wondrous kites and toys with clocks
And little engines with tracks to run on
And telephones of cans and thread.
I played the cornet and painted pictures,
Modeled in clay and took the part
Of the villain in the "Octoroon."
But then at twenty-one I married
And had to live, and so, to live
I learned the trade of making watches
And kept the jewelry store on the square,
Thinking, thinking, thinking, thinking,—
Not of business, but of the engine
I studied the calculus to build.
And all Spoon River watched and waited
To see it work, but it never worked.
And a few kind souls believed my genius
Was somehow hampered by the store.
It wasn't true. The truth was this:
I didn't have the brains.

Rebelliousness, which is one of the most recurrent states in the book, is also that which best shows the stature of Lee Masters. Not one rhetorical phrase, not one gesture, but weary souls who retire within themselves at the end, and let themselves be overwhelmed by, or disappear in, the world. This girl's epitaph seems to me especially notable:

ROSIE ROBERTS

I was sick, but more than that, I was mad
At the crooked police, and the crooked game of life.

So I wrote to the Chief of Police at Peoria:
"I am here in my girlhood home in Spoon River,
Gradually wasting away.
But come and take me, I killed the son
Of the merchant prince, in Madam Lou's,
And the papers that said he killed himself
In his home while cleaning a hunting gun—
Lied like the devil to hush up scandal,
For the bribe of advertising.
In my room I shot him, at Madam Lou's,
Because he knocked me down when I said
That, in spite of all the money he had,
I'd see my lover that night."

And finally the last one:

PAULINE BARRETT

Almost the shell of a woman after the surgeon's knife!
And almost a year to creep back into strength,
Till the dawn of our wedding decennial
Found me my seeming self again.
We walked the forest together,
By a path of soundless moss and turf.
But I could not look in your eyes,
And you could not look in my eyes,
For such sorrow was ours—the beginning of gray in your
 hair,
And I but a shell of myself.
And what did we talk of?—sky and water,
Anything, 'most, to hide our thoughts.
And then your gift of wild roses,
Set on the table to grace our dinner.
Poor heart, how bravely you struggled
To imagine and live a remembered rapture!
Then my spirit drooped as the night came on,
And you left me alone in my room for a while,
As you did when I was a bride, poor heart.
And I looked in the mirror and something said:
"One should be all dead when one is half-dead—
Nor ever mock life, nor ever cheat love."
And I did it looking there in the mirror—
Dear, have you ever understood?

This epitaph gives the measure of Lee Masters' art. Twilight creatures at the twilight hour, memories, shades, reticences of narration, everything unites to create a scene that has about it almost a supernatural aura. It is something like a faery scene by an English romantic poet, by a Yeats. But—and here is the importance not only of Lee Masters but of all the new American literature—this aura is completely realistic, it is a shudder of pain, it is, above all, a human creation, which is part of an austere moral poem, while those others, the English romantics, and not only they, have with their faeries done just a little too much childish romping.

HERMAN MELVILLE

The current importance of this nineteenth-century writer who is only now coming into his real reputation can be wholly condensed in a contrast. We, children of the nineteenth century, have in our bones the lust for adventures, for the primitive, for "real life," which is a consequence and aftermath of culture, and which frees us from complications by creating a poultice for a paltry little decadent soul, sick from civilization. Our heroes still go by the names of Rimbaud, Gauguin, and Stevenson. Herman Melville, on the other hand, first lived genuine adventures, the primitive; he was a noble savage first, and he entered the world of thought and culture later, bringing to it the health and balance acquired in real life. Now, that for some time we have felt a great need for rebarbarization is plain: there is evidence enough in the renewed desire for travel, for sport, for cinema, for jazz, fascination with the Negro, and all the other things which are tedious even to recall, and which in a synthetic word we call antiliterature. All this is doubtless wonderful. But it is the manner that is offensive, since it seems to me that, in the antiliterature fervor, there is a tendency toward the kind of primitivism which is tantamount to imbecility. Weakness, I mean, for surely it is cowardly to flee from complications to a simplistic paradise which is, after all, so understood, only one of the many refinements of civilization. I was mistaken, a moment ago: our hero is not Rimbaud, or Gauguin, or Stevenson, it is human wreckage. Melville's ideal, on the other hand, culminates in Ishmael, a sailor who can row with his illiterate mates half a day after a sperm whale and then retire to the masthead to contemplate Plato.

It is no accident that Herman Melville is an American. These latest arrivals on the cultural scene, who are held responsible, by its guardians, for the rebarbarization of our ideals—and, all censure excluded, with reason—have much to teach us in this connection. They knew how to renew themselves, passing their culture through an experience primitive and real, not, as is the sorry way with us, repudiating one term for the other, but rather, through what is called life, enriching, disciplining, and empowering their literature. "Thinking meant nothing at all unless it was done with the whole body." This is clearly an American saying, and to this ideal the whole literary tradition of the States, from Thoreau to Sherwood Anderson, consciously or unconsciously tends, succeeding in the creation of powerful individuals who spend a good number of years in uncultivated pursuits, experiencing and absorbing, and who then devote themselves to culture, reelaborating the experienced reality in reflections and images which, by virtue of their dignity and their tranquil and virile frankness, have something of that balance we normally call Greek. With such writers, we are far indeed from the artificial paradises which welcome our fastidious neobarbarians at the ends of the earth.

Herman Melville entered life delicate and estranged. At age nineteen it appears that he was already scribbling. Then unexpectedly the sea: four years of accidents and friendships, whaling, the Marquesas, a young lady, Tahiti, Japan, sperm whales, some reading, many reveries, Callao, Cape Horn—and then at Boston, in October 1844, there steps ashore a man's man, sunburned, experienced in the vices and worth of men. "A thoroughly developed gentleman is always robust and healthy," Melville would say later, in the midst of a life of straitened means, of melancholy, and also of sickness. For the American people, however practical, are not in fact so superficial and facile as you might think. Almost all the American writers who best carried over into literature this ideal of balance and serenity worked in the midst of terrible difficulty, in the midst of poverty and sickness. Walt Whitman—let him stand for them all—paralyzed for nearly twenty years and chronically broke. Even these experiences of hardship contributed to their sense of reality, concentrating their thought, rendering them more aware. The health of these people—apart from the body which is the condition of it—lies in the vitality and freshness of spirit that outlive physical fitness.

And not even Melville, in the long literary career that began the day he debarked at Boston, would allow himself to be a prolific writer, somewhat facile and superficial, which would have been understandable to expect of a man who had traveled a lot and seen exotic places. In several books he would fail, in the midst of heroic efforts, even when it was a question (as in the case of *Mardi*) of magnificent defects of growth, and in other books (such as *Moby-Dick*) he would tortuously write and rewrite until he ruined his own health; in this respect he was the true brother of so many others among his "barbarous" compatriots, who were on the contrary among the most insatiable and craftsmanlike workers of the century. Melville is really a Greek. Read the European attempts to get away from literature and you feel more literary than ever, you feel small, cerebral, effeminate; read Melville, who was not ashamed to begin *Moby-Dick*—that epic poem of savage life—with eight pages of citations, and who then goes on discussing, quoting still more, playing the role of a scholar, and your lungs are expanded, your brain is expanded, you feel more alive and more manly. And, as with the Greeks, no matter how dark the tragedy (*Moby-Dick*), so great are the tranquillity and purity of its chorus (Ishmael) that we always leave the theater exalted in our own capacity for life.

Herman Melville is thus above all a man of letters and a thinker, who began as a whaleman, a Robinson Crusoe, and a vagabond. Surely we have an example of his way of being primitive from reading the fragments of this eulogy of life at sea which are made to the author by a sea wolf, known and admired by all as Noble Jack, who in leisure moments is in the habit of reciting to his worthiest comrades selections from the *Lusiads*. It is the barbarian, the literary discoverer of the South Seas, who writes:

> Ay, Camoens was a sailor once! Then, there's Falconer, whose "Shipwreck" will never founder, though he himself, poor fellow, was lost at sea in the *Aurora* frigate. Old Noah was the first sailor. And St. Paul, too, knew how to box the compass, my lad! mind you that chapter in Acts? I couldn't spin the yarn better myself. Were you ever in Malta? They called it Melita in the Apostle's day. . . . There's Shelley, he was quite a sailor. Shelley—poor lad! . . . he was drowned in the Mediterranean, you know, near Leghorn. . . . Trelawney was by at the burning; and he was an ocean-rover, too! Ay, and Byron helped put a piece of a keel on the fire. . . . And was not Byron a sailor? an amateur forecastle man. . . . I say, White Jacket, d'ye mind me? there never was a very great man yet who spent all his life inland. . . . I'll swear Shakespeare was once a captain of the forecastle. Do you mind the first scene in *The Tempest?* . . . A snuff of the sea, my boy, is inspiration . . . for, d'ye see, there's no gammon about the ocean; it knocks the false keel right off a pretender's bows; it tells him just what he is, and makes him feel it, too.
>
> (*White-Jacket*)

It is necessary to have clearly in mind of what this culture of Melville consists, which plays so great a part in his work. It would be an error to think that this man was formed by the eighteenth century. As is true of the entire literary world of the States from 1830 to 1850 (Poe, Emerson, Hawthorne, Alcott, etc.), the eighteenth century, however well known, has been transcended, at least in its most eighteenth-century aspects. Benjamin Franklin no longer interests anyone but patriots. The tastes of this "golden day" are related to the English tastes of a Coleridge, a Keats, a Shelley: for them the great century is the seventeenth, that intellectual seventeenth century which also includes at least a good half of the sixteenth. However, while a Keats or a Shelley was seeking in the early seventeenth century more than anything else a stylistic and lyric tradition, the Americans, and Melville above all, discovered deeper sources there, not only in the recollection of the historical crisis from which the colonies originated, but in the need of spiritual references to the powerful thirst for interior freedom, for the beyond, the unknown, which gave life and traditions to these colonies.

These New England Americans were great readers of the Bible (and, be it noted, the authorized English version is 1611). In *Moby-Dick* its presence is felt at every step, not only in the sound of such names as Ahab, Ishmael, Rachel, Jeroboam, Bildad, Elijah, and all the others, but in the continuous spirit of Puritan sublimity and harshness, which makes of what might otherwise seem a scientific "tale of terror" à la Poe a dark moral tragedy where the catastrophe is the work not of a human or natural force, but of a monster named Leviathan. The curious thing is that Melville maintains toward the Bible an unprejudiced rationalistic attitude. There is in *Moby-Dick* a most entertaining chapter on "Jonah Historically Regarded." And it is here that the seventeenth century truly enters the scene.

Meanwhile, the effervescent tone of the new scientific and philosophical language which at that time was in the process of formation, mixing Latinizing solemnities with the nervous, almost vernacular bursts of the new sensibility, often reechoes in the pages of the Puritan whaleman. If I were sure that he had read him, I would say that Melville drew most of all from Giordano Bruno. But it is difficult to deal with such matters. And in any case the writers with whom he can be more reliably connected are Rabelais and the Elizabethans. There is the delight of the catalog, of verbal abundance, and of *vivez joyeux:* sometimes Melville even manages burlesque quotation. The Elizabethans gave him those flashes of style, those solemnly Latinate images, that love of contrasts, which end, however, by being rather imaginative bravura than anything else. But Platonizing rationalism, especially that of the English essayists, which meanders beneath all the intellectual manifestations of the century, was the source where Melville drank most. Naturally, as he read the Bible, he also read Plato and, I imagine, from first to last, the neo-Platonists and the mystics. But the historical form in which these tendencies presented themselves to him was unquestionably that of the English seventeenth century. Sir Thomas Browne was one of his spiritual fathers, not only a master of style, and that sentence of the *Religio Medici,* "this visible world is but a picture of the invisible, wherein as in a pourtract, things are not truely, but in equivocall shapes" (Part I, section xii), not only reappears in the epigraph to "Rime of the Ancient Mariner" by Coleridge —another essential key to the understanding of *Moby-Dick*— but returns in this same work on the lips of Captain Ahab who, although mad, is philosophically of the author's school. Now Sir Thomas Browne, besides being a kind of mystical magician, is also a subtle rationalist and contrives certain reasons for the Christian faith which, by some dogmatic people, have caused him to be taken for a heretic or an atheist.

Such is the attitude of Melville. In the early works on the Polynesian theme—*Typee* (1846) and *Omoo* (1847)—and in *White-Jacket* (1850), he is still a hearty young man who likes sun and wind and beautiful native girls and adventures with happy endings: and, if one may say so, he is still unconscious. But open *Mardi* (1849), and finally *Moby-Dick* (1851), and you find the much vaster experience of a man tormented by insoluble problems to the degree that it issues, as in *Mardi,* in allegorical oddities and botches, and, in *Moby-Dick,* in some exacerbated oratory, but especially in a brilliant and subtle investigation, in a scientific labor of examination, of meditation, of continuous quotation, somehow to resolve the mystery.

Now it would take much more than one might wish to give here a clear summary idea of *Moby-Dick;* still, while inviting the reader, who might yet need it, the sooner to abandon on his part any article whatever in order to read the book itself, I will say that it is about the cruise of the whaler *Pequod* through three oceans, the Atlantic, the Indian, and the Pacific, nominally (as the owners think, and at the time of embarkation, the crew) to hunt sperm whales; but in effect, as in a sort of *Walpurgisnacht* stage setting, Captain Ahab reveals his intention and swears the crew to kill and to take revenge upon the White Whale (Moby Dick), a sperm whale famous for ferocity, which on a previous cruise had mutilated Ahab. The substance of the book—which also bears for subtitle *The Whale*—lies entirely in a miraculous balance between minute technical details, which realistically describe the customs of the sea and of the whale fishery, and the mad supernatural passages of signs, predictions, radiating like an aura from the grim and biblical Ahab, all caught up in his monomania. Because, for the crew of the *Pequod,* Moby Dick, through the magnetism he has for their commander and through the legendary terrors that arise from his feats, as they are reported along the way by the ships they encounter, confusedly threatens to become a myth with the usual hidden allegories.

But enigma remains enigma and the White Whale, with all that is connected with him, disappears, so that nothing is known about him, or, more precisely in this context, everything. For Melville is no jack-of-all-trades who makes use of an aura of mystery every time an effect is needed and he no longer knows what to say. Melville is precisely one of those Doubting Thomases of reason who illuminated the seventeenth century. As the Apostles were not willing to believe in the Resurrection, in *Moby-Dick* Melville does not want to believe in the spirit-spout, one of the aforementioned supernatural passages;

he does not want to believe that Fedallah, the head of Ahab's Malays, really smells of sulphur; he does not want to believe in the prophecies; and even the pertinacity of the sharks behind Ahab's boat he tries to explain with the fact that sharks like the meat of Malays more than any other. What remains mysterious in *Moby-Dick,* the demonism of the universe, the intelligence behind the forces of natural destruction, that invisible world of which the visible is only a portrait, all this is genuinely mysterious—given, of course, the spiritual world of the author—and a capricious critic might say that for whoever tries to explain it further there is reserved the end of Captain Ahab.

That is what happened to Melville when, having grown in confidence, he attempted in 1852, in *Pierre,* psychological analysis—as in 1849 he had attempted in *Mardi,* but more surreptitiously, metaphysical and social analysis—of the evil of the world, of contradictions in morals, of the blind wall which "butts all inquiring heads at last." Given Melville's aesthetic instinct, his culture, his preparation and experience, this "one-half of the world" had to remain a mystery, and so it did in *Moby-Dick,* and consequently *Moby-Dick* is a masterpiece. All the other books of Melville—excluding the juvenilia which ignore this problem, and a few minor works, the novellas of "The Encantadas" (1854) and "Benito Cereno" (1855)—more or less fail on the same grounds. One could say that in them the rational destroys the transcendent. A clear example of this is *The Confidence-Man* (1857), which through a kind of human comedy that takes place on a Mississippi steamboat, tries to plumb humanity, for polemical pessimistic ends, but succeeds instead in being a wordy, obscure, and heavy-handed satire. And in *Mardi*—a symbolic narrative of the wanderings of Taji, seeker of an ill-defined ideal through a Polynesia transformed at need into a sorry map with a key, where every name corresponds to a state or an institution of the Western world—the balance between the rational and the transcendent, necessary to Melville's mature art, fails precisely because of the allegorical and philosophical vivisection made of the "enigmas." So that, despite the South Seas setting (as in *Typee* and *Omoo*), despite innumerable happy passages of satire, parody, and philosophic dialogue, despite the elegance and precision of certain symbols, the book is on the whole a failure. But, as I said, there is the excuse that these are defects of growth and that *Mardi* beat the pathway to *Moby-Dick.*

On the other hand, there is no excuse for *Pierre; or, The Ambiguities,* a psychological attempt to demonstrate that society and the universe are badly contrived, that moral perfection itself can't conduce to goodness, that an act of abnegation (the marriage Pierre contracts with a natural sister, in order to give her a home) becomes, under the pressures of society—and of life—a monstrosity (the more than fraternal love of the pair). It is the malevolence of the White Whale which tries to clarify itself in these analyses that leave nothing more to the supernatural, to the mysterious, with the usual imbalance: the style becomes convulsive, the inspiration epileptic and fragmented, the sense of proportion fails, and on certain pages still cut in the old style there extends a swamp of verbal preciosity, false notes, and ingenuities, which are not only wearisome but after all simpleminded. Truly the book seems written by Ahab.

As with all great works, you might never finish analyzing *Moby-Dick* in order to discover new points of view, new meanings, and new importances. I have mentioned what seems to me the most definitive meaning of the story in the foregoing discussion, but, for all that, how is the reader to take Melville's austere legendary manner, that tone which is not at all exhausted in the pleasures of the imagination but is altogether impregnated with severe moral thoughtfulness? Or the nervous and solemn tranquillity, sometimes ruffled by a mischievous smile, with which the realistic chapters of description, information, and discussion flow? But especially it is that continuous feeling of immensity, of the superhuman, toward which the entire book converges, in a miracle of construction, through which little by little the gay and Puritan atmosphere of the beginning and then the "scientific" atmosphere of the long central explications, become fused in the last part in a spirit of brilliant and powerful recklessness, almost mythical, just as the name and fame of the White Whale, kept offstage until the conclusion, grow until they loom over and fill all settings, actions, and thoughts. To show the whole construction of this work would require a page-by-page commentary for all the six hundred pages of the book, nor could one otherwise exhaust the wealth of techniques and effects in *Moby-Dick.* Here I can only give two diverse excerpts in order to illustrate what I have said.

In the first, notice the life mysterious and swollen with omens which Melville knows how to derive from his ocean:

> But, at last, when turning to the eastward, the Cape winds began howling around us, and we rose and fell upon the long, troubled seas that are there; when the ivory-tusked Pequod sharply bowed to the blast, and gored the dark waves in her madness, till, like showers of silver chips, the foam-flakes flew over her bulwarks; then all this desolate vacuity of life went away, but gave place to sights more dismal than before.
>
> Close to our bows, strange forms in the water darted hither and thither before us; while thick in our rear flew the inscrutable sea-ravens. And every morning, perched on our stays, rows of these birds were seen; and spite of our hootings, for a long time obstinately clung to the hemp, as though they deemed our ship some drifting, uninhabited craft; a thing appointed to desolation, and therefore fit roosting-place for their homeless selves. And heaved and heaved, still unrestingly heaved the black sea, as if its vast tides were a conscience; and the great mundane soul were in anguish and remorse for the long sin and suffering it had bred.
>
> Cape of Good Hope, do they call ye?
>
> ("The Spirit-Spout")

And in the second notice the clear mastery—hardly at all disturbed by the action—of the epic narrator who knows that he has in hand a subject of which the imagination sooner tires than the possibilities of poetry are exhausted:

"Pull up—pull up!" he now cried to the bowsman, as the waning whale relaxed in his wrath. "Pull up!—close to!" and the boat ranged along the fish's flank. When reaching far over the bow, Stubb slowly churned his long sharp lance into the fish, and kept it there, carefully churning and churning, as if cautiously seeking to feel after some gold watch that the whale might have swallowed, and which he was fearful of breaking ere he could hook it out. But that gold watch he sought was the innermost life of the fish. And now it is struck; for, starting from his trance into that unspeakable thing called his "flurry," the monster horribly wallowed in his blood, overwrapped himself in impenetrable, mad, boiling spray, so that the imperilled craft, instantly dropping astern, had much ado blindly to struggle out from that phrensied twilight into the clear air of the day.

And now abating in his flurry, the whale once more rolled out into view; surging from side to side; spasmodically dilating and contracting his spout-hole, with sharp, cracking, agonized respirations. At last, gush after gush of clotted red gore, as if it had been the purple lees of red wine, shot into the frighted air; and falling back again, ran dripping down his motionless flanks into the sea. His heart had burst!

"He's dead, Mr. Stubb," said Daggoo.

"Yes; both pipes smoked out!" and withdrawing his own from his mouth, Stubb scattered the dead ashes over the water; and, for a moment, stood thoughtfully eyeing the vast corpse he had made.

("Stubb Kills a Whale")

There remains the minor Melville, the early works more substantially autobiographical: *Typee,* primitive and idyllic life among the cannibals of the Marquesas; *Omoo* (The Wanderer), travels through the Society Islands, among settlers and natives; *White-Jacket,* Melville's life in the navy aboard a man-of-war, a deluge of characters and of comic types, a liberal education in life and human nature. To the reader who has not read them, these books might even seem to be those barbarian books which at all costs the whaleman—no longer Puritan but pagan—must surely have written.

I have already quoted a passage from *White-Jacket* that indicates to what extent Melville was uncultured even in these works, but it can always be objected that *White-Jacket* is

1850—that is to say, after *Mardi*—and that undeniably the Polynesia of the early books has a much more innocent air than that of the settings in the three novels just discussed, *Mardi, Moby-Dick,* and *Pierre.* This fact, as I might add, is especially obvious in *Mardi,* where although Yillah (the feminine ideal whom the protagonist pursues among the islands) is not only the Fayaway of *Typee,* that is, innocence and natural grace in person, but is a metaphysical embodiment of these and similar related virtues, nevertheless the story—which opens the book —of the calm at sea, the idyll with Yillah in the paradise of Mardi, and some of the subsequent landscapes that smile among the allegories, possess the same unassuming, unsophisticated tone of the best pages in *Typee* and *Omoo.* This incongruity between the two parts of *Mardi* is just what marks the difference between the minor Melville and the Melville of *Moby-Dick* and *Pierre.* The intrusion of new intellectual preoccupations in the guise of allegory, of a baroque psychology, and of mystery was to be the ruination but also the glory of the future Melville. The minor works, at which we are presently glancing, ignore these preoccupations, they ignore the mystery of the universe, the so-called problem of the White Whale. In this way they avoid the obstreperous failure of a *Pierre,* but they are also precluded from the miracle of a *Moby-Dick.*

Therein lies the difference. But the spiritual relationship with the rest of the oeuvre is still to be found in the tone, even in its simplicity learnedly aware of itself, and thereby the more dignified. The fascination of the three books is doubtless (referring to the simple first impression) in their continuous conversation, in that effervescence of intellect, of caricature, and of *joie de vivre,* against a background of immense serenity like glints from the ocean they describe. Still, come to think of it, just what is *Typee* but a continuous comparison, established by a man of completely occidental education, between certain customs and certain aberrations of his own civilization and the firsthand experience of a simpler civilization, but one essentially more peculiar, not wanting, that is, in pure ostentation? And what are *Omoo* and *White-Jacket* but a free and easy comedy, where a sort of magisterial Dante smiles in good humor and friendliness upon his comrades, but deep down is different from them and, on the islands of the archipelago, forms a learned little clique with the Doctor, or, on the man-of-war, with Noble Jack (the Camoens man), judging all the others, including big shots, consul, captain, and commodore, with the calm assurance of the man who "has studied"?

But I don't want to leave the impression that Melville was an inhuman pedant, wholly bent on offering (under the pretext of adventures) his doses of bookish powder. Simply, it is a pleasure to observe how when he writes Melville remembers the books he has read and quotes them like a man, estimating them without false modesty at their true worth and always half smiling through his beard. In him this humorous style of the scholar promenading through the oceans is, as it were, the surface layer of an intellectual structure of extraordinary and comprehensive profundity. Thus a paragraph of *Moby-Dick* concludes (there having been suspended at the side of the *Pequod* the head of a sperm whale; another, of a right whale, after a hunt, is hoisted on the other side):

> As before, the Pequod steeply leaned over towards the sperm whale's head, now, by the counterpoise of both heads, she regained her even keel; though sorely strained, you may well believe. So, when on one side you hoist in Locke's head, you go over that way; but now, on the other side, hoist in Kant's and you come back again; but in very poor plight. Thus, some minds for ever keep trimming boat. Oh, ye foolish! throw all these thunderheads overboard, and then you will float light and right.
>
> ("Stubb and Flask Kill a Right Whale")

Finally, Melville left collections of verses, of his old age or almost, verses in meter and with rhyme. But what could the prose stylist who wrote *Moby-Dick* and "The Encantadas" possibly say in meter? There is something in all this which resembles Whitman. Herman Melville has more in common with the sage of Camden than rebellion against the petty realities of his day, a mixed English and Dutch ancestry, and the dates of birth and, practically, of death (1819–1891 and 1819–1892). They also share a slow dissolution in old age, in weariness, and in isolation, accompanied by the rather melancholy spectacle of a kind of writing that has become a habit, the "garrulity" of the last years, which desperately tries to recapture a note from the oceanic symphonies of their prime. Walt Whitman was luckier; after the persistent optimism of his creative years, he found in sorrow and in disappointment one last thin vein of minor poetry, of "heavenly death," of twilight resignation. Melville, sadly, had already expressed, in his great sea legend, sorrow, the unknowable beyond, and nothing; and so he found himself at the end, exhausted and empty, with nothing more than a refrain at heart:

"Summer and winter, and pleasure and pain
And everything everywhere in God's reign,
They end, and anon they begin again:
Wane and wax, wax and wane:
Over and over and over amain . . ."

"Since light and shade are equal set
And all revolves, nor more ye know;
Ah, why should tears the pale cheek fret
For aught that waneth here below.
Let go, let go!"

("Pontoosuce")

It is the only aspect of these late poems that arrests the reader. And Whitman had already said, in his catastrophic syntax:

Myself through every by-gone phase—my idle youth—old age at hand,
My three-score years of life summ'd up, and more, and past,
By any grand ideal tried, intentionless, the whole a nothing,
And haply yet some drop within God's scheme's ensemble—some wave, or part of wave,
Like one of yours, ye multitudinous ocean.

("By That Long Scan of Waves")

PREFACE TO MOBY-DICK

To translate *Moby-Dick* is to put yourself in touch with the times. The book, hitherto unknown in Italy, has through half the past century secretly inspired the greatest books of the sea. And for several decades English-speaking readers have been returning to Melville as to a spiritual father, discovering in him, enormous and vital, the many themes an exoticising literature had later reduced, over half a century, to vulgarity.

Herman Melville was born in New York in 1819 of an old and upper-class family, and he died in New York in 1891, after having passed through government clerkships, impoverished, unappreciated, alienated. But his misfortunes are not the issue. It is the usual fate of the great men upon whom the professors are pleased to expend their tender eloquence, only to treat their own contemporaries in the most old-fashioned way. In any case, Melville's misfortunes had a part in *Moby-Dick,* and are therefore welcome. We must also remember the four years of youth spent on whaleships and men-of-war, in the Pacific, in the Atlantic, amidst hunts, typhoons, calms, adventures of Inferno and Arcadia, all material that was later filtered, with a slow labor of assimilation, in the works. There is

Arcadia in *Typee,* in *Omoo,* in *Mardi,* stories inspired by the months of his life lived with cannibals on an oceanic island. The Inferno is in *White-Jacket*—that frank and merciless journal of life aboard a man-of-war—and in *Pierre,* a grim moral story which is a failure, and which serves to show at what price and with what efforts the author of *Moby-Dick* achieved a masterpiece.

The reader must first of all bear in mind that more than eighty years have passed since this book was first published. The intellectual climate from which it issued is by now entirely forgotten, even in America, and every time that somebody wants to elucidate one of its works, a meticulous effort of re-creation is required. Fortunately, two representative writers from this same climate are quite well known in Italy, however crudely; things will go more easily once we think of them. It has often been felt that Herman Melville is a kind of fusion, and, with it, a transcendence, of Edgar Poe and Nathaniel Hawthorne. In the present instance, *Moby-Dick* is, in a thousand pages, a short story à la Poe, with all his construction, his reasoned effects of terror, his mathematical bent, even in language; and, at the same time, it is one of those moral analyses of sinners, of rebels against God which, expressed in an eloquent and sparkling style for the purpose of a sermon, perhaps connects *The Scarlet Letter* rather to the history of Puritanism than to the history of poetry.

At that time in America, or more precisely in New England, recently achieved national stability sharpened the desire for a native culture, a tradition. This desire, which was to be the chronic problem of the States, and which even today provokes so much contempt in Europe toward those parvenus of culture, is, on the contrary, the sign of the nobility of their effort, and of their destiny. For to possess a tradition is less than nothing: it is only in searching for it that you can live it.

Melville and his contemporaries sought it, good Puritans that they were, in the century of the religious wars in England, in that century of visionaries, of theological pamphleteers and interpreters of the Bible from which America was born. Even Poe, who in his writings is sufficiently nonreligious, ate too heavily of the sixteenth and seventeenth centuries, addressing himself mainly to the writers of magic and of the occult, and to the Platonists. All people who were not displeasing even to Melville. But *Moby-Dick,* reasoned out and technical as it is, scores above all for its biblical inspiration. In it the Whale, after all the classifications and the scientific and archeological terms, remains more than anything else "Leviathan."

Read this book, keeping the Bible in mind, and you see how what might have seemed to you a curious novel of adventures, a little long, to tell the truth, and a trifle obscure, reveals itself instead as a genuine and original sacred poem, in which neither heaven nor earth has failed to lend a helping hand. From the first quoted extract, "And God created great whales," to that of the epilogue, from Job, "And I only am escaped alone to tell thee," the whole atmosphere is of Old Testament solemnity and severity, of human prides humbled by God, of natural terrors which are the direct manifestation of Him. Those opening chapters, which have even seemed superfluous to some readers, on the somber tombstones of New Bedford whalemen and on the sermon about Jonah, are instead an essential part of the story: the horror of the whaleship which is associated, at its first appearance, with the sacred Puritan terror. Surely there is nothing superfluous, with respect to the tone of the book, in this epitaph:

SACRED
TO THE MEMORY
OF
JOHN TALBOT,
Who, at the age of eighteen, was lost overboard,
Near the Isle of Desolation, off Patagonia,
November 1st, 1836.
THIS TABLET
Is erected to his Memory
BY HIS SISTER.

But, it is only that biblical interpretation I was speaking of which can make us understand how everything is harmonious, and how everything is in its place, as every phrase is in a story by Poe.

The entire book is so conceived. The opening, a little reckless and burlesque, the most realistic part of that life, which culminates in the figure of the cannibal harpooneer, more loyal and sincere than any white man; the entrance of the ship, as covered with ivory and tusks as a barbaric king, adds a new shudder to the adventure; then, another burlesque interlude (the shipowners Bildad and Peleg) of a simple humorousness but full of meaning, since Bildad, so much a miser, is reading the Bible, and Peleg, so good-natured and irreverent, will speak for the first time of Ahab; the enlistment, and then the mysterious rumors about Ahab (it is notable that neither Ahab nor the White Whale appears until the last possible moment, and that both are preceded and accompanied by whispering and apprehensive rumors). And the names that go along with this tragedy, how often they have already recalled the Bible! Ishmael, Jonah, Elijah, Bildad, Ahab ("and the dogs licked up his blood"). It must immediately be remarked that Ahab is not a man like all the others. It is his lot to rave, to fast, to stay awake, to talk like Hamlet, and, from time to time, to issue encyclicals to heaven. Whoever seeks to find in him a created psychological and realistic character can go ahead and seek.

Lord knows who first put in circulation this misleading tale about characterization! It seems to me that a book can admit only one character, the author, and that all the reflections, all the partial descriptions of settings and characters which contribute to the construction, should be referred to him. Ahab is not a real man, by virtue of the simple fact that he is the counterpart of Moby Dick, whose psychology, I presume, nobody will pretend to explain. And the universe surrounding the two, which helps to fix them in their positions, is a universe so tortured and biblical it is sheer luck that it yielded so relatively calm a type. All the other characters in the book are parts, parts of construction, and all serve their ends, not because they were once "true," but because they are harmonized in their form—which might even be false in real life—with the particular imaginative setting in which they are found, and detached from which they would lose all consistency. Fedallah, for example, the mysterious head of Ahab's Malays, snatched from his seat and carried off to a reckoning with reality, might even strike a malicious reader as an early version of the Indian *vendicatore* in *Giovanotti non esageriamo.* The only *human* personage of the book has to be Ishmael, in his function of the eye that judges in a first-person narrative, in short, in his function as author.

It is more profitable to say a word about the mystery of Moby Dick and all the supernatural evidences that accompany him. There is nothing to be discovered behind the White Whale. Its fearful significance lies precisely in the fact that it signifies a void, a nothing, a brute force, or an unknowable agent (which comes to the same thing). And here it is appropriate to observe with what subtlety Moby Dick is kept in the shade until the end, even when he is being discussed through the book in all his manifestations; with what skill he is brought gradually to loom over the scene by means of his *effects,* as recounted by the ships that have met him. You could continue such an examination through the whole book, and discover how logical, how calculated, every chapter is, every sentence, every phrase. The continuous supernatural atmosphere that transfigures even the most impartial and scientific of the author's investigations is only a way of expressing, through every secular aspect of culture, the biblical spirit of the overall conception.

Something needs to be said of this culture, since it shows us the way to the other half of Melville's world. Opening the book to those pages of initial "Extracts" on the whale, the reader may still be surprised and may think that at least these pedantic quotations can be skipped, for these at least are superfluous. No, not even these. The fascinating list of references, fished for in all "the long Vaticans and street-stalls of the earth," and the etymologies, from more than a dozen languages, which precede it, serve to bring the reader to that level of universality, to accustom him to that secularized atmosphere of learned discussion, which will be the structural basis, sometimes humorous and sometimes heroic, of all the future chapters. This is a curious thing in *Moby-Dick* and in Melville: although it is a work inspired by the experiences of a nearly barbarian life at the ends of the earth, Melville is never a clown who sets out to pretend that he too is a barbarian and a primitive, but, dignified, courageous, he is not afraid to reelaborate that pristine life by means of all the knowledge of the world. And truly I think you need less courage to front a sperm whale or a typoon than to take the chance of passing for a pedant or a "man of letters." In his thanks to the Sub-Sub-Librarian, whom he pretends has supplied him the quotations, Melville commiserates him as one of that "hopeless, sallow tribe which no wine of this world will ever warm; and for whom even Pale Sherry would be too rosy-strong"; he commiserates him in the usual jocular tone of a man whose acquaintance with life goes well beyond the "long Vaticans and street-stalls," and who knows that the greatest poems are those told by unlettered sailors on the forecastle (cf. "The Town-Ho's Story"); he knows all this, and jokes about it, but he is not ashamed to show himself as he is, a sailor who has studied: a man of letters.

PREFACE TO DARK LAUGHTER

Toward the end of the last century the author of this book was a young worker who used to spend his evenings sprawled on a broken-down bed in a furnished room—a very badly furnished room—idly reading about almost anything in the world. Outside was the noise and smoke of Chicago, on the way to becoming the greatest industrial center of the Middle West. When he was tired of reading, or when there was no more light, young Anderson—he tells us these things himself in *A Story Teller's Story*—would close the book and begin to daydream. Or he would leap from the bed and go out to wander through the streets, among factories and workingmen's houses, meditating on what seemed to him only ugliness and vulgarity. He came from parts even worse, as he recalled, from the provincial interior of Ohio, where at a stroke the poor and peaceful life of those jerry-built and half-agricultural towns of his childhood had been struck by an earthquake and by a great fever: industrialism, the race for riches, the "efficiency rush," the cult of the hard-driving heroes, coarse speech, machinery, all that passes for contemporary America.

His Ohio childhood had taught Sherwood Anderson only to read and write and that life is hard. Children of immigrants, or nearly, those families constituted a generation that lived in Ohio—as others lived in Nebraska, in Illinois, in the Dakotas—without even the pride of conquest felt by the earlier pioneers, who have now vanished; without any reason for loving it; without interest in it; they lived there because life had thrown them there. Empty prairies, a few rivers, wooden villages, everywhere corn and cabbages and a flat oppressive immensity. In Chicago, where he went to seek his fortune, young Anderson found only another kind of desolation: men who toiled, who fought for advantage, who elbowed each other out of the way, dreaming of a soft life; gathered in shacks as temporary as those in the country, with a language equally banal, and no longer with even the solace of free horizons—to say nothing of the implacable misery, such an exploitation of the human animal as has never been seen since the days of slavery.

Young Anderson read. He read everything, from Caesar's *Commentaries* to Renaissance biographies to Walt Whitman's *Leaves of Grass.* His imagination played wild tricks on him. Even for a long time afterward, when he was more mature, more a man, it befell him that mild-mannered Americans were transformed by hallucination into cinquecento lordlings, and he found himself writing out long lists of meaningless words, for no other reason than to give vent to the intoxications of his loneliness. But even the most obvious absurdities that Sherwood Anderson was able to imagine or envisage as a worker in the mushrooming city take importance from an idea. The idea is the same that lends fascination and power to this book, *Dark Laughter,* written by Anderson at age forty-nine in 1925, when Chicago and the whole United States had already pulled themselves together and taken a calm deep breath, as if to forget the chaotic period of their origins. The idea and the problem are the same that have tormented and continue to torment the artists and the men who are going to matter in the future history of the United States. The worker Sherwood Anderson used to ask himself: What on earth is the meaning of this enormous nation made up of the leavings of all the nations; which lives, sweats, curses, and continually renews itself; which has no beauty, no memory, no nothing, except a boundless appetite for life and opportunity, and which in its highest expressions so far has only known how to ape the worn-out gestures of Europe, and to varnish itself anew with the most counterfeit splendors of Europe? Anderson searched for an answer to this question in all the books, in all the facts, in all the experience that reached his awareness—and not only as a worker, but also later on, when he was a soldier, a stableboy, an advertising man, and a businessman—and from the chaos of glimmering intuitions and shapeless experiences he knew how to derive only daydreams, interior transfigurations of that endless movie that played before him, until little by little the daydream, the transfiguration of reality, seemed to him the same as the sense of his own life and the way through which he might give a meaning, a justification, to the States also.

And then another problem loomed, the other tremendous task that Anderson took upon himself for his country: How to express this new historical actuality, how to re-create in the imagination, how to order afresh, how to construct (since for Anderson art meant bringing order and pattern where once there was chaos) the scattered material constituting this unprecedented nation of half a hundred nations? Where was there an artistic and spiritual American tradition? Before him stood Europe—you can see it in the book—ancient, mature, knowledgeable: expert first in life, and then as a consequence in art, where the creators live close to their lands, to things, with simplicity, with humility, *listening*. In America, on the other hand, the artist was an *isolato,* a stranger to his own country; the country itself seemed only veneer, and pretentiousness was the word for the whole way of life. What did America know of the humility and earthiness of the great artists of the European past? So it appeared at first glance to Anderson; and, moreover, in America there were the machines, the easy riches, and the Puritanism—everything that stifles the artist and life.

But—and here lies the importance of *Dark Laughter* and of Anderson in general, as distinguished from certain would-be American artists who expatriate themselves in Europe—in America as well blood runs in the body, in America as well there are instincts, passions, vital labors, and not merely works of efficiency; it is possible to invent images and to construct worlds. And what is more, at least one American had achieved such a creation. Those pages on Mark Twain, author of *Tom Sawyer* and *Huckleberry Finn,* poet of the good life of the heartland on the big river, are like the lightning flashes of Anderson's national discovery. There is vitality in America as in Old Europe. There is eternal nature, there are songs, the river, love, laughter, the Negroes: dark laughter. And with redoubled energy Anderson sings a hymn to Negro life, to the humility of the Negroes in the face of things, because in this way he can strike off the white man's shackles of pride and of Puritan materialism.

This book is centrally concerned with the creation of a new ideal of American life in the Bruce-Aline couple, and with the tragedy of the distortions of pride and rhetoric in Fred and Bernice. Bruce and Aline build this new life of theirs slowly, sorrowfully, as the obscure worker did in Chicago, as they confront the Negroes and Europe, imbuing themselves with the lowly and healthy sensuality of the former and with all the anguished and profound wisdom that Anderson sees in us old ones. Consequently, the novel is entirely made of the imaginative sensibility in which Anderson discovered his America: the characters exist and speak to us with that dreamlike and luxurious immobility which is the life Anderson wants to teach America. They tell themselves with their own slow laboriousness, directly before us, as if they themselves were seized by the pleasure and by the need *to exist imaginatively* or not to exist: to be only a chaos, a nullity, a nation made of banal optimism and lies.

O. HENRY; OR, THE LITERARY TRICK

The excellent selection and translation that Giacomo Prampolini has recently made of O. Henry once more puts before us one of the most perplexing personalities in American civilization. Until now this capricious storyteller has been a little too much maltreated by us in illustrated magazines and the like, which every so often for want of news had recourse to his Thousand and One Nights. From there, translating by ear, cutting and reinforcing, they continued to dig out disconcerting and almost anonymous pages that for good or ill imported a little animation into the midst of the tired lucubrations of our storytellers. But this vulgarization of O. Henry has served a little too much to disseminate among us what in America, where at least they read O. Henry in whole volumes, is by now a widespread inclination: the suspicion that not all that dazzle of inexhaustible invention is of good quality, that O. Henry wrote too many brilliant stories. And at the twenty-first you shout "Stop!"

Still, who hasn't shouted "Stop!" at some point with any short-story writer? These things are like the collections, which were once the fashion, of epigrams and sonnets: they have to be read in small doses, on the installment plan. Except that on these terms O. Henry would be tiresome, not insofar as he was a short-story writer but insofar as he was a writer. His tales, we are now sure, end with a bang because they are *empty,* because they give us only the surface of reality, because in them puns and paradoxes are the trumpery of a barren inner life.

Let it lie—for the time being—the "inner life": I can personally declare that to read O. Henry is almost always entertaining and that you always have before you a most sympathetic kind of man who, as full of brio as one of his many heroes is full of whiskey, continues to recount little anecdotes and witticisms and adventures with a cordiality and a spirit quite exceptional. So that those who deplore the fact that O. Henry has created nothing, no *character,* are at least this one time wrong: a character there is, alive and speaking—even too much so—who at every moment has something of his own to say and (outrageously!) almost always says it well: O. Henry or, to his friends, William S. Porter. A writer even needs to be a little listened to, and if anyone had said to O. Henry's face that he wanted more aching humanity, or whatever, O. Henry surely would have told him to take it easier, because to insist on certain fixed ideas is to risk losing what little there is and to vex the soul over what little there is not.

For O. Henry is honest. He doesn't try to bluff, as so many of his most attractive characters do, but from the early pages of his best book there is revealed the trick, if trick it is and not rather the unconstraint of every artist worthy of the name:

> " 'Tis contrary to art and philosophy to give you the information. . . . The art of narrative consists in concealing from your audience everything it wants to know until after you expose your favorite opinions on topics foreign to the subject. A good story is like a bitter pill with the sugar coating inside of it. I will begin, if you please, with a horoscope."
>
> (*Cabbages and Kings*)

Now such a confession, made where it is made, can clarify O. Henry's intentions and techniques. In the first place, he does not come from a cultivated society like that of a Maupassant or a Flaubert, and therefore he never dreamed of longing for an impersonal, realistic, or primitivistic literature. Not that one recipe is preferable to another, what is important is to say something with whatever recipe one uses; but it is useful in the present instance clearly to distinguish O. Henry from those others, because too many readers, not finding him another Maupassant, have rejected him. O. Henry clearly tells you that he conceives the short story as an oblique discourse, as a series of verbal and structural tricks that seem and are not, as a continuous comment and byplay of the narrator to the actions of his characters: so much so that, as I have already noticed, the character who leaps most conspicuously to the eye in his pages is the speaker himself.

Now this fact has deeper and more complicated roots than may appear. And if the reader of O. Henry's stories would think again about the cultural atmosphere from which these stories are drawn, many things might seem to him obvious that presently annoy him, since the singular nature of the writer was entirely conditioned by the intellectual moment into which he was born. He who thinks back to the only period of American letters at all well known in Europe, the period—naturally—of Poe and Emerson (1830–1850), will seem to find himself in absolutely another continent than the one of which O. Henry gives us an idea in his writings (1900–1910). The earlier writers had made a center of New England, nourishing themselves on European culture, while vitally transforming it, and ignoring all the great territory and the future variety of races in the nation. Then the polished speech of the best seventeenth-century English traditions prevailed, together with the writer shut in a tower to ruminate the almost invariably occult sciences, in short, the Puritan province of anti-Puritan rebels, aristocratic and isolated.

Consider instead the age of O. Henry. Roosevelt's administration has yielded its fruits: America is henceforth a single nation from the Atlantic to the Pacific, no more Puritan than necessary, with the business of the chosen people to excuse its conquests and its new riches, and it is so sure of itself, so much a "melting pot," that it dares to receive, in order to naturalize them, even the Armenians, the Negroes, and the Chinese. The cultural centers are henceforth spread through the whole huge country, with the consequence of a slight diffusion of forces, although a youthful simplicity—and not a poverty—of spirits just then sings its most frenetic hymns to the élan vital (Jack London). There no longer exists an Athens of the United States, New England. The new centers are as numerous as the free play of races, released from every traditional barrier, knows how to produce: California, with Norris and London; the Center (Chicago), with Sinclair and young Dreiser; New York, finally, with the first movies and O. Henry. One thing of immense significance and importance is the transfer of the movie studios from New York to California that occurs just at the end of this period, around 1912. The whole American territory is henceforward in this way crisscrossed by intellectual currents. Before, up to 1850, America was divided into two worlds: the New England which thought and wrote, and the West, broadly understood, from the Alleghenies to Wyoming and Texas, which conquered and broke ground. The former, slightly skeptical literary aristocrats, the latter, rough illiterate Puritans who chewed tobacco and fought with their fists.

This is not the place to tell the whole story. Suffice it to say that from Poe you get to O. Henry through a half century of revolutions: trappers, miners, new cities, new states, the War of Secession, contingents of Germans, Swedes, Italians, territorial conquests, industrialism, oil and coal, corn, the unrestrained love of life as life, no longer as mere thought or the printed page. The earlier New England dies because the English public forgets how to read, it no longer knows English well, much less the polished English of Boston or of Richmond, or it no longer has time to waste getting to the bottom of philosophies. The powerful body of the U.S.A. begins to look about restlessly, to search for writers who speak of its own life, who will tell it something more than the gambling parlor, or the racecourse, or the fever of work. But clearly: something more, not something different. The new short stories that triumph in all the American newspapers from 1870 to 1910 are essentially humorous or anyhow full of action and "suspense." It has been rightly said that the America of this period seeks in its short stories a duplicate of the emotions of Luna Park: distorting mirrors, chutes, thrills, clowns, sleight of hand, laughs, and noise. Elsewhere, mainly in the states of the Center (Illinois, Indiana, Wisconsin), there will be coming into vogue gloomy novels of which the whole interest consists in the attempt to give a grayly faithful reproduction of reality: from this vogue Dreiser will issue. Immediately after, from 1900 on, there enters the picture the tastes for the social question, these too more life than literature: the rally, the strike, the organization, the revolution (*The Iron Heel, Metropolis*)—tastes that persisted into the renaissance of 1912, which will be essentially a deepening of the new cultural centers on the basis of more vital problems. But this is another subject altogether.

Finally, this literature that culminates in the "prince" O. Henry has a new characteristic: it is a dialect literature. It is a curious kind of dialect, because we Italians imagine dialects to be local and we would have looked for a dialect literature rather from New England. But in America dialect is the colloquial speech spoken by everybody in contrast to the cultivated and upper-class English taught in the schools. Localisms (as they say over there) hardly exist in their language. Reasons: the youth of this language and the intricacy of communications which from one day to the next causes the New Yorker to live in California or the Great Laker in Florida. The dialect quality of the short stories from Mark Twain to O. Henry comes from the need to speak to a rather democratic public (miners, sometimes), and in any case always to speak to a bourgeoisie which tends toward solidity and wants to understand and to recognize itself in its newspapers. Because of course from Mark Twain to O. Henry all the literature that lives is journalistic.

It would certainly be sufficient, then, if it happened in poetry as in the cultivation of fruit, to define the O. Henry story as the final literary manifestation of that period which begins with the crude pages of anonymous miners where witticisms in dialect serve to cheer up a people rather trivial and rather tired of existence. But, I repeat, poetry is not a cultivation of fruit, and it has not yet been proved that a fine example of it arises from long seasons of selection and grafting; and so it happens that, having explained everything, it is just as well to begin again at the beginning and to ask yourself once more: Has O. Henry really "created something"? Or is he not rather the "light," "skin-deep," "fantastic" writer, and in the worst sense of these words?

Let us return to those previously mentioned *Cabbages and Kings*. This is a sequence of stories collected in a novel. The setting of the novel is already a proof of the new American cosmopolitanism and imperialism. A tiny Central American republic, Anchuria, easily turned upside down by factions, governed by Spanish types full of high-sounding words and essentially understood in terms of their own "price." O. Henry's hand begins to reveal itself in the way this material is treated: the events are seen from Coralio, a small town of many huts and a few residences on the shores of the Spanish Main, where American consuls and traders in bananas, rubber, and shoes assist the various local revolutions, helping them along, and attributing to them so much importance as is permitted a discreet citizen of the United States who doesn't too much believe in the politics even of his own country. The atmosphere of the tale is above all the blessed indolence of that sky and sea, where everything can happen and nothing does, or at least it leaves no trace and, as a president falls or a Christian dies, a hundred thousand of them could fall and die and the novel would always be the same. Therefore, its nature is excellent, clearly revealed in episodes, in varied stories.

O. Henry's notorious "insufficiencies," then, the mechanical quality of the action, the cerebral trickiness in the presentation of the adventures, must surely be quite plainly exemplified in this free and easy plot. Thus, for example, the fact that the two characters (President Miraflores and the actress Isabel, who have run off with government funds) imminent in and dominating the whole book, are not at all who they are thought to be, and that they have succeeded in escaping, and that their place is taken by two Americans, a father and daughter who have run off from their country with money from an insurance company, this fact appears to be only an oddity, a contrivance of the storyteller's, the final unexpected happening desired by the slightly gross and childish taste of the public. But after it has been said that the book is entirely constructed like the ordinary card castle, what has been revealed about O. Henry except what he himself has already too hastily confessed? The lecture can be repeated for each of the chapter-stories which comprise the book and for every other story that O. Henry ever wrote. We always find in him, in the structure of the action, these overturnings of values, these paradoxes, these bluffs.

And it is at this point that the critical labor ought to begin. What else should we expect from O. Henry but mechanical actions? And this (you observe) would be a defect as fatal as the other defect of even the most highly esteemed writers, in whom are found only fragments of observations, of "material," and the plot, the construction, is either nonexistent or virtually nonexistent. But reread, with that kind of goodwill indispensable to any enjoyment, the whole book of which I speak —for the moment the hundreds of other short stories aren't important—reflect upon it a bit, keeping in mind the historical bases that have been alluded to, and I am convinced that in the end you will begin to have doubts about the theory of the trick. Have we not before us instead a bizarre and delightful kind of writer who sees the entire universe as a bewildering stylization and who, far from inventing paradoxical adventures because he doesn't know what to say, feels these paradoxes as the very substance of life?

In sum, specific historical conditions suggested to O. Henry a certain taste, a certain manner; they imposed upon him, in short, certain themes. And why can't O. Henry have made of these themes poetry, a genuine creation, that is to say, a genuine *form* of a lively sensibility, of what can seem to be but is only at the beginning a trick (the aforementioned substitution of characters in *Cabbages and Kings*), which makes an expression or a myth of the oddity and relativity and fundamental illogic of life?

The conclusion of the adventure of Miraflores and Isabel is characteristic; saved by a misunderstanding, they are constrained by it to live far away a fictitious and almost unbearable life. To conclude the various strands of the narrative, O. Henry has imagined a little cinematographic scene.

The Writing on the Sands

SCENE—*The Beach at Nice.* A woman, beautiful, still young, exquisitely clothed, complacent, poised, reclines near the water, idly scrawling letters in the sand with the staff of her silken parasol. The beauty of her face is audacious; her languid pose is one that you feel to be impermanent—you wait, expectant, for her to spring or glide or crawl, like a panther that has unaccountably become stock-still. She idly scrawls in the sand; and the word that she always writes is "Isabel." A man sits a few yards away. You can see that they are companions, even if no longer comrades. His face is dark and smooth, and almost inscrutable—but not quite. The two speak little together. The man also scratches on the sand with his cane. And the word that he writes is "Anchuria." And then he looks out where the Mediterranean and the sky intermingle, with death in his gaze.

This would not seem to be cerebral. The account of the tricks in the action has naturally been exaggerated. Many times the O. Henry story presents only a humorous stylization of persons or events, or it is odd only in the way that a scene is perceived, an opinion expressed, or the "philosophy" of an event treated.

So we enter the real heart of the question about the "inner life" of O. Henry, a question that seems to me potentially answered already by the reply to the charges of trickery in the action—except that many people still, especially in America, boldly distinguish action from characters, characters from style, style from content. Returning therefore to the point of departure, imagine O. Henry as the American night owl who has lived by his wits in all the states of the Union and beyond, carefully saving up that little store of riches which enables him to rattle off stories in an unsophisticated manner, with his legs under the table, all his impressions of existence condensed in jokes, in demonstrations of good-humored paradoxes, and sometimes moved by a friendship, by a sorrow, by a distant sacrifice; only thus shall we have before us his "inner life."

All O. Henry's heroes, we notice, are from New York, or are provincials like himself who have made their apprenticeship through the whole nation and now end, experienced and tolerant, taking shelter in old Manhattan. These persons are naturally not monuments of psychology or pyres of passion: the language that describes them, the tone of the narrative, the good-natured intimacy of the recollection, everything conspires to reduce their proportions, everything casts over O. Henry's events a faint shade of jest and of "philosophy"—which permits no creative luxury, in the usual sense of the term. In the act of conversing, O. Henry describes his types; he gives a brush stroke and then he stops—looks at the listener—makes an observation on some related memory, winks with his eyes, gestures with his hands, changes the position of his cigar, gives another brush stroke. For it is not O. Henry's intention to describe such or such another character in the name of humanity; he tends simply to represent in the most direct and least pedantic way possible a memory of something incredible, curious, paradoxical. The principle that comprehends and unifies all his narrative art is just this, the knowing exposition of something intellectually unusual, bizarre, "queer."

In his characters no other law of unity can be found. There are vagabonds in his stories, genial burglars, melancholy gentlemen, drunks, naive young girls, déclassé nobles, politicians, prostitutes of strict morals, young wives desperate out of spite, assassins: all the scum and the flower of the American melting pot. But not even the appeal of the beatitude of liquor and indolence, the most common appeal in O. Henry's world, is sufficient to pull together all these characters. Their real affiinity consists only in their strangeness, in the oddity of their cases, sometimes sad, almost always cheerful, more or less resigned. Here is an example. A decayed gentleman, reduced to sleeping on park benches and living by his wits, feels winter coming on in New York. What to do? Get himself arrested; three months on Staten Island; security and repose. How to get himself arrested? He tries to eat in a hotel, without money: they don't denounce him, they beat him. He tries to smash the window of a store, and accuses himself: they don't believe him. He tries to molest a lady: it's all right with her! Evening comes; the "never-wuzzer" walks desperately through the streets. He stops before a church. He hears an organ. Gentle thoughts begin to stir in his head, childhood, illusions, the abject present. He has made a decision: tomorrow he will go to work and reform his life. At that moment, a policeman, finding him without identification papers, arrests him. Three months of "repose" on Staten Island. A thousand such tales could be recounted. No need to be afraid of declaring that O. Henry exists precisely and only in the ironic and slightly saddened sense of these paradoxical contrasts.

Granted this conception of the short story—conversation at a bar about some chance happening—it follows that often it will be worth less as a unified story than in certain of its details: a mocking image, an exclamation, a scene. This, if anything, is somewhat the defect of O. Henry, not that other one of the "superficial action." You could make a whole list of expressions, of descriptive mannerisms, of crackling, well-turned, and quite fantastic epithets: their only defect is that they can be so easily detached and collected. But for every one of these slightly external expressions, how many there are of the utmost felicity! This can be verified on simply opening the book, and I don't at the moment want to go big-game hunting after flies. O. Henry's is a real "dialect" humor; no manufactured language would sustain so volcanic and continuous a shower of phrases and words. In this respect, O. Henry is truly the Rabelais of the United States. And also in the taste, half erudite and half popular, for letting things go, for living happily—la Devinière, the liquor store—the two resemble each other.

As Rabelais seems to be, more than an initiator, the necessary crown of a gauloise tradition that was essentially expressed in the fabliaux, so O. Henry concludes the carefree youth of the American novella or "short story." This genre (let us for once speak of genre), born with those early humorists of the miners' newspapers, carried to its first triumphs by punsters and dialect writers as notable as Artemus Ward, had already excelled in the hands of Mark Twain and Bret Harte, the self-conscious pioneers of the new literature no longer New England but national. At the time of O. Henry, everyone was writing short stories. The genre had enriched itself; no longer were there only stories half-humorous and half-sentimental, but Ambrose Bierce, for instance, was imitating, rather badly, in fact, Poe, and Jack London—everybody knows what Jack London was doing.

O. Henry found his tone with a rare security and timeliness. Of all the writers of his age, it was he who was also best suited to speak in a newspaper to the *whole* nation. The veins of the bizarre and of the cosmopolitan which he opened up were, even in their precise delimitations, the most comprehensive epitome of every short fictional effort up to then achieved in the new nation. And if although, like Rabelais, he concludes a period in such a manner that no one had to stop there any longer and other tendencies were developed, still, the language, the expressive American spirit, by him exemplified and justified in a thousand ways, could easily survive him. And indeed the generation that follows O. Henry—Dreiser, Lindsay, Lee Masters, Sandburg, Lewis, Anderson—doesn't forget the lesson, and in its work of interpretation and re-creation of the U.S.A. will carry to its termination the great linguistic revolution, and this will definitively become in new hands the conscious instrument for an exploration entirely intellectual.

JOHN DOS PASSOS AND THE AMERICAN NOVEL

I don't think I was alone in Italy in searching out my first Dos Passos because of the shock felt at seeing *Folla.* The word was going around that King Vidor had drawn the film from *Manhattan Transfer.* And of *Manhattan Transfer* they were reporting great wonders as the most original and most profound book written in America in those years. It seemed odd that so good a film had already been a good novel. In these translations, either you destroy on the screen what was once perfect on the page, or else from the vacuity of an indifferent book an entirely new structure is created. It is impossible to decant poetry.

The answer is really very simple: King Vidor had done one thing and Dos Passos quite another. Nor does the question lie in the matter of "tone"—cinematographic tone or novelistic tone; a work of art can't change genre as you change your suit, precisely because genre is not costume but the very body of the work. *Manhattan Transfer* and *Folla,* despite certain episodic similarities in their material, are two different worlds, each with its own laws, its own problems, and its own criteria. Against the vague and half-apocalyptic background of New York, *Folla* shows a pathetic clerk, rebel in the name of a bourgeois right to life, and around him there stand his wife and children. Everything else—hospital, office, street, theater, relatives, the crowd—is like a rude natural force, like the thunder and lightning which make all the more dear the little comforts of a warm living room and a completed task. *Manhattan Transfer,* on the other hand, juxtaposes about twenty characters, following the narrative lines of each, never or almost never mixing them. There is no longer a frustrated bourgeois hero from whose point of view to contemplate the metropolis, but this metropolis vivisected into all its frustrated people of every class; each one is scrutinized in isolation from the others, living within himself, but somewhat in the way that a piece of flesh just cut from a body might live in a laboratory. An air of scientific experiment. Moreover, the characters live their lives of bitterness and of hopes, and somebody dies, and others exit (as they entered) from the narrative, with a great monotony, in all their metropolitan variety. For, beyond the fact that all these people are more or less the same figure of a man or a woman with similar thirsts for money, fame, and ease, this monotony seems also to be increased by Dos Passos' curious style, composed of visual or olfactory sensations, and of snapshots of gestures and of words —always the same, these words, in their multiplicity of quite faithful reproductions of everyday language—and which carefully excludes any direct presentation of the state of soul of the characters. These states must be inferred from the brilliant representations of the screen and sound track. And they are inferred very well indeed, but their human complexity suffers from the exigencies of external clarity of that cinematographic style, which makes everything seem like an irritating technical attempt to create only a new face of realism. In short, the work is not only not that tragic everyday epic of all New York which Dos Passos thought it was, but it doesn't even get beyond being a heap of picturesque fragments.

A reading of the works prior to *Manhattan Transfer* (1925) tells nothing more. *Three Soldiers* (1921) is the usual bitter tract against war—though it has the merit of being, I think, the first of its kind in America; *A Pushcart at the Curb* (1922) is the usual collection of impressionistic poems, full of stylistic daring and lacking in construction. And these two works are the most representative. However, since *Three Soldiers,* Dos Passos has had in mind a whole epic: the chaotic fever of struggle and quest among the great masses of the metropolis (and for him the whole world is metropolis) who suffocate in material and spiritual narrowness, where isolated victories count for nothing, surrounded as they are by innumerable defeats.

After further experiments and attempts at playwriting which don't concern me here, Dos Passos returns to this conception in his latest volumes, *The 42nd Parallel* (1930) and *1919* (1932), which is a continuation of it. He still tells his story by means of the juxtaposition of characters, of whom each reproduces, in his isolation from the others, the same drama with the same environmental relationships. Every character therefore excludes all the others of the book, without hierarchical construction. Poetically, no one is of use to anyone else, although Dos Passos is persuaded that he is giving, through their contemporaneity and "chaotic' juxtaposition, the atmosphere of a world "chaotically" tormented. And therefore you tire of reading one after another all these series of episodes. But the curious thing is that, for the first time in Dos Passos, all these replicas of the same world are alive, despite their common pattern, and with whichever character you begin, the first character will always be the most effective.

The cause of this paradoxical fact is that Dos Passos has chosen no longer to tell his story by means of episodes but through passages of biography, and this is a matter of no small consequence, for even though these passages of biography are all interwoven with episodes of the spirit and of the style which informed *Manhattan Transfer,* still, their mere exposition—no longer restricted to the impressionistic vignettes, but carried forward from event to event through the same character, so that every instant of their lives throws light on their past and future—begets a certain perspective, organizes a human experience. Dos Passos has a way all his own of narrating the biographies: he begins at the birth, or about that time, and never leaves empty a single day of his protagonist; sometimes he condenses—"in that month," "in that year"—but nothing is ever passed over in silence. In Dos Passos you never find those sudden leaps, those implications so convenient for ending a chapter with dramatic effect and commencing another with such ease. Even in the interruptions made inevitable by the various interweavings of the biographies, Dos Passos doesn't take advantage in this way; he begins again exactly where he left off and goes on from there. And then, at the end of the book, each biography is suddenly cut short, without apparent reason. To *1919* Dos Passos can add when he likes another volume, taking up again the characters who didn't die on him, or inventing as many others as he wants. There is up to now in the two volumes no structure that could take damage from it. The presumed structure is left to the crisis of the war, which gathers together all the characters, men and women, and serves them as a common field of unhappy experiences. But this external event constructs nothing in reality, since it has nothing substantial to teach the characters that they don't already know in the bourgeois and revolutionary prewar world.

Moreover, it so happens that these protagonists get all mixed up in the reader's memory. They are constructed with a prodigious episodic richness, and not even a chance incident of theirs escapes the author, but this richness, which ought greatly to diversify them, ends by decomposing them all in a multicolored, never-changing panorama of the chaos of the world and of the inadequacy and injustice inherent in contemporary society. Joe Williams is an ignorant young man, who goes to the dogs among sailors and exotic whorehouses, while dodging the draft and living his life; and then he is killed in France in a brawl with a Senegalese officer in a cabaret of

Saint-Nazaire. Well, all the protagonists of the biographies—young university students cursing the horror and stupidity of the conflict; open-minded, intellectual, and, for all their freedom, unhappy Red Cross volunteers; workers and agitators maltreated by life and by "capitalism"—all repeat in themselves the experiences of Joe Williams: each one dodges *his* draft, his annihilation by the machine of a society which could end by falling to pieces in the catastrophe of the war. The individual events, the external data, the thoughts expressed by the characters, these differ from one to another; but the problem, the drama, is in all of them the same. So much so that in reading you ask yourself sometimes which of the characters Dos Passos is talking about. Moreover, in every episode of each one there is the drama of the whole life of this man or this woman, which is thus the life of all.

Sometimes the scene becomes comic, but it is a comedy of clenched teeth; beneath that absurdity, that laughable incongruity, there is always somebody who is moaning or cursing; and impassive Dos Passos renders it all with the same objective, rapid, journalistic air of the man who is in a hurry and can't waste his time searching for effects. This is his power.

Joe and Del left in a taxicab a feller he knew drove and everybody threw rice at them and Joe found he had a sign reading Newlywed pinned on the tail of his coat and Del cried and cried and when they got to their apartment Del locked herself in the bathroom and wouldn't answer when he called and he was afraid she'd fainted.

Joe took off his new blue serge coat and his collar and necktie and walked up and down not knowing what to do. It was six o'clock in the evening. He had to be aboard ship at midnight because they were sailing for France as soon as it was day. He didn't know what to do. He thought maybe she'd want something to eat, so he cooked up some bacon and eggs on the stove. By the time everything was cold and Joe was walking up and down cussing under his breath, Del came out of the bathroom looking all fresh and pink like nothing had happened. She said she couldn't eat anything but let's go to a movie . . . "But, honeybug," said Joe, "I've got to pull out at twelve." She began to cry again and he flushed and felt awful fussed. She snuggled up to him and said, "We won't stay for the feature. We'll come back in time." He grabbed her and started hugging her but she held him off firmly and said, "Later."

Joe couldn't look at the picture. When they got back to the apartment it was ten o'clock. She let him pull off her clothes but she jumped into bed and wrapped the bedclothes around her and whimpered that she was afraid of having a baby, that he must wait till she found out what to do to keep from having a baby. All she let him do was rub up against her through the bedclothes and then suddenly it was ten of twelve and he had to jump into his clothes and run down to the wharf. An old colored man rowed him out to where his ship lay at anchor. It was a sweetsmelling spring night without any moon. He heard honking overhead and tried to squint up his eyes to see the birds passing against the pale stars. "Them's geese, boss," said the old colored man in a soft voice. When he climbed on board everybody started kidding him and declared he looked all wore out. Joe didn't know what to say so he talked big and kidded back and lied like a fish.

(*1919,* "Joe Williams")

The poetry of Dos Passos consists in this dry way of perceiving and rendering things. "Joe couldn't look at the picture"; and this is the most introspective moment in a whole narrative of external facts, inexhaustibly and clearly expounded, with a detachment that is a moral judgment. Through his horror of tracing out psychological flourishes in a life where it is enough to observe and accumulate a thousand appearances for evaluation, Dos Passos has made himself a style, in his humble objectivity so rich with delicate nuances: they are half gestures, half words, or colors, odors, sounds, full of meaning, joyful in their expressive energy; a novelty in American literature, unless you go back to certain pages of impressions, to the jottings scattered through the prose and verse of that other enfant terrible of this culture, namely, Walt Whitman.

"Say, Mac, we better keep out of sight if we want to hop that freight. There's some friggin' mean yard detectives on this road." "All right." They walked off a hundred yards into the young growth of scrub pine and birch. Beside a big greenlichened stump Mac stopped to make water. His urine flowed bright yellow in the sun, disappearing at once into the porous loam of rotten leaves and wood. He was very happy. He gave the stump a kick. It was rotten. His foot went through it and a little powder like smoke went up from it as it crashed over into the alderbushes behind.

(*The 42nd Parallel,* "Mac")

The women did the loading. After a while they started coming up one gangplank, each one with a huge green bunch of bananas slung on her head and shoulders; there were old black mammies and pretty young mulatto girls; their faces shone with sweat under the big bunchlights, you could see their swinging breasts hanging down through their ragged clothes, brown flesh through a rip in a sleeve. When each woman got to the top of the gangplank two big buck niggers lifted the bunch tenderly off her shoulders, the foreman gave her a slip of paper, and she ran down the other gangplank to the wharf again. Except for the donkeyengine men the deck crew had nothing to do. They stood around uneasy, watching the women . . . scratching themselves, shifting their weight from one foot to the other; not even much smut was passed. It was a black still night, the smell of the bananas and the stench of niggerwoman sweat was hot around them; now and then a little freshness came in a whiff off some cases of limes piled on the wharf.

(*1919,* "Joe Williams")

The German offensive was on, the lines were so near Paris the ambulances were evacuating wounded directly on the basehospitals. All night the stretcher cases would spread along the broad pavements under the trees in fresh leaf in front of the hospital; Dick would help carry them up the marble stairs into the reception room. One night they put him on duty outside the operating room and for twelve hours he had the job of carrying out buckets of blood and gauze from which protruded occasionally a shattered bone or a piece of an arm or a leg. When he went off duty he'd walk home achingly tired through the strawberryscented early Parisian morning, thinking of the faces and the eyes and the sweatdrenched hair and the clenched fingers clotted with blood and dirt and the fellows kidding and pleading for cigarettes and the bubbling groans of the lung cases.

(*1919,* "Richard Ellsworth Savage")

The reason why this impressionistic and moral sensibility achieves a poetic consistency only in these last two volumes is that here it is submitted to the narrative expediency of the biographies. It is difficult to find in these a passage of pure description. The pages are all permeated with events and you understand at the end how all fragmentary quality is overcome by the abundance of human experiences which are packed into the protagonists. This impressionistic material is now the flesh and life principle of the characters, and not an end in itself. Besides, there are in the novel sections where Dos Passos wanted to amass, for the purpose of intermission, whole handfuls of pure impressions, rendered in an avant-garde, open-dended, and literary style. These are the sections—between one part and another of the biographies—entitled "The Camera Eye," where the author gives in a page or so a kind of free-verse view of his *own* impressions at the time of the various events going on in the novel; but here also, among some moments excessively cerebral and, from the mania for immediacy, obscure, are pages that bear comparison, for richness and seriousness of experience, with the best narrative pages.

at the Gare de l'Est they're singing the *International* entire   the gendarmerie nationale is making its way slowly down Magenta into stones whistles bits of iron the *International*   Mort Aux Vaches   Barricades we must build barricades   young kids are trying to break down the shutters of an arms shop   revolver shots an old woman in a window was hit (Whose blood is that on the cobbles?) we're all running down a side street dodging into courtyards concièrges trying to close the outside doors on cavalry charging twelve abreast firecracker faces   scared and mean behind their big mustaches under their Christmastree helmets

at a corner I run into a friend running too Look out   They're shooting to kill and it's begun to rain hard so we dive in together just before a shutter slams down on the door of the little café   dark and quiet inside a few working men past middle age are grumblingly drinking at the bar   Ah les salops   There are no papers   Somebody said the revolution had triumphed in Marseilles and Lille   Ça va taper dure   We drink grog americain our feet are wet   at the next table two elderly men are playing chess over a bottle of white wine later we peep out from under the sliding shutter that's down over the door into the hard rain on the empty streets only a smashed umbrella and an old checked cap side by side in the clean stone gutter and a torn handbill L'UNION DES TRAVAILLEURS FERA

(*1919,* "The Camera Eye" (40))

Always the seriousness and splendor of little, real things, and, even though sometimes the inspiration seems to be a great event—the Armistice, strikes, mass meetings—the narrative never abandons the living annals of the protagonists, their sorrows, their pettinesses, to lose itself in generalities. Despite Dos Passos' social and revolutionary interest in large-scale events, his typical character remains always the vagabond worker, the "working-class companion," who knocks himself out to find some reason in it all, and fails to do so, and his life passes among the many-colored—and therefore, even if tragic, hopeful—experiences that we have seen.

The last quotation puts before us perhaps the most interesting side of Dos Passos' personality. All his books are obviously tendentious representations of the fight that he sees being fought out with class consciousness, in our century, between labor and capital. And there is no doubt which side he takes. Enough, to give yourself an idea of it, to recall the sections of the two last volumes entitled "Newsreel," periodically recurring between one and another portion of the biographies. They are collections put together from newspaper clippings, snatches of popular songs, slogans, passages from speeches, and so forth, of about the time at which the various "Newsreels" occur among the biographies. They are short *sottiseries* of capitalist hypocrisy and rhetoric, of the culpable disorientation of the bourgeois world during and after the war. Naturally, they don't have much to do with art, but in certain selections, in certain juxtapositions, there is revealed an implacable criticism which can be worth many iambics and many epodes.

CALIFORNIA JURY QUICKLY RENDERS VERDICT AGAINST SACRAMENTO WORKERS

'Tis the final conflict
Let each stand in his place
The international party
Shall be the human race

BOLSHEVISM READY TO COLLAPSE SAYS ESCAPED GENERAL

the French Censor will not allow the Herald to say what the Chinese Delegation has done but that there is serious unrest it would be idle to deny. Men who have been deprived of the opportunity to earn a living, who see their children crying for food, who face an indefinite shutdown of industries and a possible cessation of railway traffic with all the disorganization of national life therein implied, can hardly be expected to view the situation calmly and with equanimity

BRITISH TRY HARD TO KEEP PROMISE TO HANG KAISER

it is declared the Coreans are confident President Wilson will come in an aeroplane and listen to their views. A white flag set up on Seoul Hill is presumed to indicate the landing-place

(*1919,* "Newsreel" XXXVIII)

But Dos Passos is a remarkable artist. Instinctively, he has almost always excluded from the fictional world of his major works any explicit thesis. There he confines himself to representing, and pure poetry rewards him with the extraordinary polemic value of his characters. In the story, Dos Passos never with his own mouth enunciates critiques and programs: he contents himself with listening to his heroes. And he even has the confidence sometimes to reveal with a half smile the weaknesses or follies of burning revolutionaries, whom in certain other gloomier places he goes so far as to support with his own emotion.

Big Bill talked about solidarity and sticking together in the face of the masterclass and Mac kept wondering what Big Bill would do if he'd got a girl in trouble like that. Big Bill was saying the day had come to start building a new society in the shell of the old and for the workers to get ready to assume control of the industries they'd created out of their sweat and blood. When he said, "We stand for the one big union," there was a burst of cheering and clapping from all the wobblies in the hall. Fred Hoff nudged Mac as he clapped. "Let's raise the roof, Mac." The exploiting classes would be helpless against the solidarity of the whole working class. The militia and the yellowlegs were workingstiffs too. Once they realized the historic mission of solidarity the masterclass couldn't use them to shoot down their brothers anymore. The workers must realize that every small fight, for higher wages, for freespeech, for decent living conditions, was only significant as part of the big fight for the revolution and the coöperative commonwealth. Mac forgot about Maisie. By the time Big Bill had finished speaking his mind had run ahead of the speech so that he'd forgotten just what he said, but Mac was in a glow all over and was cheering to beat hell. He and Fred Hoff were cheering and the stocky Bohemian miner that smelt so bad next them was clapping and the oneeyed Pole on the other side was clapping and the bunch of Wops were clapping and the little Jap who was waiter at the Montezuma Club was clapping and the sixfoot ranchman who'd come in hopes of seeing a fight was clapping. "Ain't the sonofabitch some orator," he was saying again and again. "I tellyer, Utah's the state for mansized men. I'm from Ogden myself."

After the meeting Big Bill was round at the office and he joked everybody and sat down and wrote an article right there for the paper. He pulled out a flask and everybody had a drink, except Fred Hoff who didn't like Big Bill's drinking, or any drinking, and they all went to bed with the next issue on the press, feeling tired and flushed and fine.

(*The 42nd Parallel,* "Mac")

But all these heroes constitute so many arguments of revolutionary polemic precisely insofar as the author views them with objectivity, and through the absence of any theoretical conclusions—catastrophic or cathartic—on the part of their chronicler. On the whole, the world of Dos Passos is a collection of samples, of failed, corrupted, destroyed, or coerced individuals in contemporary society, without the possibility of any end to their daily tragedy. And it is this disorientation of theirs, this inescapable suffering, which affects us more than many sermons.

Only once in the biographies does Dos Passos clearly give way to his feelings. I refer to the story of Ben Compton, self-taught intellectual and Communist, whom "capitalistic society," after persecutions and brutality, ends by hounding into prison. One might like to conclude that this biography is only a pamphlet, yet even here the humanity of the character is surprising. During a patriotic celebration after the Armistice, Ben, guilty of having conducted a meeting, waits to be buried in jail.

Lower Broadway was all streaked red, white and blue with flags; there were crowds of clerks and stenographers and office-boys lining both pavements where he came up out of the subway. Cops on motorcycles were keeping the street clear. From down towards the Battery came the sound of a military band playing *Keep the Home Fires Burning.* Everybody looked flushed and happy. It was hard to keep from walking in step to the music in the fresh summer morning that smelt of the harbor and ships. He had to keep telling himself: those are the people who sent Debs to jail, those are the people who shot Joe Hill, who murdered Frank Little, those are the people who beat us up in Everett, who want me to rot for ten years in jail.
(*1919,* "Ben Compton")

It is necessary to clarify this lucky position of Dos Passos, who with us, too unilaterally, runs the risk of being reduced to a pamphleteering orator of the social school of Upton Sinclair, and of the Jack London of *The Iron Heel,* or to a twentieth-century intellectual formed on the European influences of futurism, fragmentism, and the *neue Sachlichkeit,* the whole thing badly mixed, and worse digested. We observe instead how these two excesses are in the process of exhausting themselves in the latest works in a significant detachment from the narrative: the first in the "Newsreel" sections and the second in "The Camera Eye." Meanwhile, the narrative pages, freed of abstractions and avant-gardism, remain the real Dos Passos, made of human understanding and immediacy and of an evaluating morality that transcends all polemic antagonism and every stylistic experiment.

In general, we Europeans too much tend to find our own sources in American intellectual phenomena, with the result of reducing a literature—which now in poetic accomplishment has, if anything, to teach us—to a clumsy exasperation of our own local motives. It is a matter of fact that America has long possessed its own rich tradition, which, moreover, is so near in time as to nourish, even when unsought, its young people, without those efforts toward a willed renaissance which too often, with us, give a tone of literature to the best-intentioned. That Dos Passos, like his fellow soldiers who experienced the war, learned something in France and in Europe is beyond dispute and entirely to his credit, granted that it is the privilege of the young to profit in a vital way from every contact with other cultures. But even with him, it seems to me that we exaggerate, overlooking the indigenous forces in him in order to search out those European influences which are the obsession of our intellectualism. Now Dos Passos is all saturated in the spirit of that American generation which came of age at the time of the world war. Beyond Upton Sinclair and Jack London, who counted of course, there is in him the essential influence of Dreiser and of Lewis who, to the polemic exposition of a badly contrived society, add the rich human interest typical of people in that society.

I said earlier that Dos Passos in certain respects resembles Walt Whitman. And this, despite the dizzy seventy-year interval between the two, should not seem an acrobatic exercise. For there is Carl Sandburg, contemporary with Lewis, who makes a bridge between them. From Walt Whitman you clearly see in Sandburg and then in Dos Passos the stylistic habit of coordinated details, impressionistic vivacity, and that syntactical freewheeling which, rather more than vocabulary, contributes toward the divergence of "vulgar American" from English. Moreover, Carl Sandburg has substituted the social problems of his own years for the apocalyptic "democracy" of Whitman, but in other respects, through sensibility, he clearly descends from Whitman. And Dos Passos, in that last group of sections in *The 42nd Parallel* and *1919*, which have no collective name, and are variously entitled "Big Bill," "Emperor of the Caribbean," "The Electrical Wizard," "Mister Veelson," "The House of Morgan," "The Body of an American," etc., repeats the oratorical and strenuous style of those two. In a way, these are biographical poems on an individual representative American, characters who dominated the political and intellectual life of the country, who are recalled in rapid strokes and, even here, almost never ironically or grossly polemic. Dos Passos looks rather at the tragedy of the man, even of his enemy (and there is always tragedy) ; and so the morality is born, not from criticisms or approbations, but simply from a rapid and severe representation. This is Sandburg:

> I know an ice handler who wears a flannel shirt with pearl buttons the size of a dollar,
> And he lugs a hundred-pound hunk into a saloon icebox, helps himself to cold ham and rye bread,
> Tells the bartender it's hotter than yesterday and will be hotter yet to-morrow, by Jesus,
> And is on his way with his head in the air and a hard pair of fists.
> He spends a dollar or so every Saturday night on a two hundred pound woman who washes dishes in the Hotel Morrison.
> He remembers when the union was organized he broke the noses of two scabs and loosened the nuts so the wheels came off six different wagons one morning, and he came around and watched the ice melt in the street.
> All he was sorry for was one of the scabs bit him on the knuckles of the right hand so they bled when he came around to the saloon to tell the boys about it.
>
> (*Chicago Poems*, "Ice Handler")

And this is Dos Passos:

> In nineteen twentyfour La Follette ran for president and without money or political machine rolled up four and a half million votes
>
> but he was a sick man, incessant work and the breathed out air of committee rooms and legislative chambers choked him and the dirty smell of politicians,

and he died,
an orator haranguing from the capitol of a lost republic;
but we will remember
how he sat firm in March nineteen seventeen while Woodrow Wilson was being inaugurated for the second time, and for three days held the vast machine at deadlock. They wouldn't let him speak; the galleries glared hatred at him; the senate was a lynching party,
a stumpy man with a lined face, one leg stuck out in the aisle and his arms folded and a chewed cigar in the corner of his mouth
and an undelivered speech on his desk,
a wilful man expressing no opinion but his own.
(*The 42nd Parallel,* "Fighting Bob")

This energy of treatment, entirely realistic, which saves the free verse of the Americans from the feeble impressionism of European free verse, is the inheritance from Walt Whitman. Rarely has he or Carl Sandburg attempted in poetry the refined ingenuities of sensation to which the content of this poetry is usually reduced in Europe. Rather than according to a musical law of phonic harmony, the Americans, following Whitman, divide their lines according to the logical law of the succession of the thoughts. This is their originality, ultimately of biblical derivation, and particularly fortunate in a nation where, from Whitman on down, poetry fatally and freely assumes an oratorical pose. As Whitman was long since saying:

Now I tell what I knew in Texas in my early youth. . . .
'Tis the tale of the murder in cold blood of four hundred and twelve young men.

Retreating they had form'd in a hollow square with their baggage for breastworks,
Nine hundred lives out of the surrounding enemy's, nine times their number, was the price they took in advance,
Their colonel was wounded and their ammunition gone,
They treated for an honorable capitulation, receiv'd writing and seal, gave up their arms and march'd back prisoners of war.

They were the glory of the race of rangers,
Matchless with horse, rifle, song, supper, courtship,

Large, turbulent, generous, handsome, proud, and affectionate,
Bearded, sunburnt, drest in the free costume of hunters,
Not a single one over thirty years of age.

The second First-day morning they were brought out in squads and massacred, it was beautiful early summer,
The work commenced about five o'clock and was over by eight.

(*Leaves of Grass*, "Song of Myself")

This last comparison illustrative of the normal blossoming from a native trunk of a writer who, like Dos Passos, has instead seemed the quintessence of the unpredictable, of the "meteoric," ought to be able to suggest a more serious orientation for studies of American art and thought, forcibly freeing them from the improvisors who presently waver back and forth presenting us those phenomena between the extremes of spontaneous generation and of senile rechewing. Meanwhile, the truth, for new America as for old Europe, is that nothing is born of nothing; and that, especially in the sphere of poetry, nothing notable is born unless inspired by an autochthonous culture or, if such can not be the case, by a culture at least seriously and definitively assimilated by the people and by the nation.

DREISER AND HIS SOCIAL BATTLE

The Americans are really sore at Dreiser. It is no longer the irritated distrust for the innovator, but the mocking contempt of people who have conquered their world. It no longer serves—as it once was enough—to remember that, if now in America they can read tranquilly and with so much subtle pleasure the adolescent and unfeeling naughtinesses of Hemingway or the dramatic indictments of matrimony by Lewisohn, in large part this is due to Dreiser's long campaign which, with the firm pedantry of a scientist, swept away the Puritan restraints. "Dreiser, the big man" makes the young people laugh. What is unpleasant is that, with the young, the old people once more turn to sneer, those who had suffered his dictatorship while champing at the bit; and now they are delighted that they can slander the "Master." And with him goes all the "fake revival," the empty renaissance of 1912, by him inspired and by Henry Mencken directed. Carl Sandburg becomes something halfway between a journalist and a writer of popular songs; Vachel Lindsay, a mental case of the jazz age, who accidentally wrote three or four strangely colored poems; Edgar Lee Masters, a nebulous and importunate moralist; Sherwood Anderson, an intellectual pauper, stammering a mysticism so fatuous that it actually begins to resemble communism.

I once remarked, speaking of Lee Masters, how it is dangerous to judge these writers on the basis of their most provincial topics of social polemic. One of them, Sinclair Lewis, for example, has been as much in America as in Europe entirely misunderstood through the mania for seeing in him nothing else than the satirist of mechanical-capitalistic civilization. It is necessary instead to insist that the Babbitts, the Arrowsmiths, and the Elmer Gantrys do not after all mean very much as caricatures of the businessman, of the scientist, or of the religionist, but overwhelmingly impose themselves upon the imagination as solid and restless figures of a society which is searching for itself and which lives by means of this restlessness.

Even Dreiser, if you look for him in his polemic intentions, now that the smoke of the twenty-year battle has vanished, seems little less of an innocent. Was there need of so great a mobilization of force in the "Revival," and of so much noise, with the flag of the *American Mercury* at its head, to bring it about that American taste might educate itself to read, calmly, about sexual matters? For then the whole affair boils down simply to this: to succeed in saying freely in America the things that are said in Europe, "on the continent." And naturally, if these writers still count for something, the reason must be sought in some depth of human vision, which can't help but appear in a literature that, for the first time in America, from the Center, where with such provincial roots it is born, intends and knows how to speak to the whole Union.

Dreiser began the campaign for liberty in art with the attempted publication of his first book in 1900. It says much about American culture of the time, to recall that *Sister Carrie,* in the author's intention, and unfortunately even in reality, was a manifesto of naturalism or, as Dreiser prefers to call it, realism. Brutal writers America had already had (London, Crane). Dreiser's intention was not only to be "brutal" in the word, in the created work of art, that is, but objectively to represent a world which lives "brutally," which is badly made. But this was also the program of Zola, pamphleteer and experimental novelist. Forty years after French naturalism, Dreiser should have been able to choose better, at least in his intentions. But in Dreiser there is even something of bad Balzac, in the heroic inventory of the settings; and all these experiences had to be gone through in America, in order to assimilate Europe and in order to find oneself after the war fresh, unprejudiced, and prepared for every more contemporary experiment. Now that some time has passed, we can see very well that *Sister Carrie* was not that cyclone that the "Revival" used to pretend, but a modest natural plant, sprung from a ground already broken by writers who imposed, on the chaos of the author's bookish European inspirations, the most suitable indigenous form. Those writers were Stephen Crane and Frank Norris: the first, a disillusioned and tragic psychologist who embroidered, in a rather hallucinated fashion, on the most common and realistic material—a title is enough: *Maggie: a Girl of the Streets;* the other, the progenitor of Upton Sinclair, public denouncer of the crimes of the great industrialists. Dreiser, describing the life, not even too immoral, of his Carrie—who ruins a successful average man of Chicago, running off with him and then abandoning him in misery in order to go on the stage—found his originality in the fact that none of the characters is evil, but life is evil. These ideas, rechewed in the novel with the fetching obstinacy of a young author, are what make the readers of 1933 laugh. The originality—what little there is of it in *Sister Carrie*—is instead, in part, in the wonder for the great city that arises, a wonder rendered by means of the wanderings of Carrie through Chicago and of her companion Hurstwood through New York, looking for work; and, in general, in the appetite for the passions observed as a vigorous spectacle of forces.

All things considered, that which in Dreiser's early works represents a regression to earlier writers of the Middle West

(Kirkland and Garland), and also to some of his most immediate influences, is the artistic impurity of his narration. Armed with a "philosophy" as simplistic as it is headstrong, and which is repeated at every turn of the page, he writes novels with the air of a man developing a scientific theory, and characters and events furnish him examples. If not *The Titan* (1914), then *The Financier* (1912), the first part of the diptych, is still infected by this manner. The protagonist, F. W. Cowperwood—the not very novel figure of the captain of industry who makes and unmakes, usurps and destroys, and finally falls under accumulated hatreds—lives through episodes, through examples, of which each one illustrates the sagacity, the cold-bloodedness, the daring, the fascination, and the other virtues of the extraordinary man. The curious thing is that all these attributes are not at all improbable—Dreiser knows what he's doing—and that Cowperwood is alive, although laboriously alive, confined in the closed atmosphere of an apology for princes. At every audacious decision, at every piratical undertaking, at every sexual conquest by this man (and there are several), Dreiser stops to note that victory goes to the most powerful, that the universe is a battlefield of impartial struggle, that good and evil are only our ideals, that every satisfaction is an abuse of power, but that on the whole the cosmic equilibrium levels all, even the victor. You observe the abuse of "chemistry" which Dreiser indulges in all his books. This word is his logos. Every abstraction is a chemism for him: thought, passion, digestion, history, art, good, evil. He said he was not a psychologist, but a biochemist.

Naturally, the play of the paradoxes and the digressive ease in every chapter, with that slovenly manner of the "essay" which sometimes even tried to be humorous—*Sister Carrie*—soon fell. Dreiser, who was ever more fixed in the idea of giving the great table of chemical reactions of the American world, understood how all that dispersion would little serve his design, which instead asks nothing but objectivity, heroic objectivity, in psychology and setting, the elements and methods of experiment. He finally achieved—by instinct, in all probability, not by reflection—that halving, that purification of his narrative vein, which would lead him to his masterpiece. Henceforth we will have two categories in his works. First, there are the essays, or tales, or miscellanies, that range from the pure theoretical treatment of ideas (*Hey Rub-a-Dub-Dub,* 1920) to the chronicle (*A Hoosier Holiday,* 1916; *The Color of a Great City,* 1923), or to the portraiture (*Twelve Men,* 1919; *A Gallery of Women,* 1929) which presents acquaintances as characters, but regarding them through the author's own autobiographical experiences, making of them symbols of lost days, and thus another chronicle. And all this part, despite the current opinion that prefers them to the novels, seems to me rather saccharine and easy, because in it the encroaching expository slovenliness strips almost all form from a world—already fragmentary in itself—entirely made up of memory, gossip, and aphorisms. Meanwhile the other category, the construction of "passional equations," self-defined in the natural right of the Titan, traversing the psychological pigheadedness of *The "Genius"* (1915)—always more free from compromises with philosophy—leads to *An American Tragedy* (1925).

Dreiser writes badly. By this I think is meant that he writes like a journalist, without feeling for the word, in set phrases and in offhand approximations. But the question is badly put. *I* think that it is precisely when Dreiser shows less feeling for the word, when he is more seized by the fact—action, speech, or passion—which, as *he* sees it, *realistically,* need not be false to daily experience, then it is no longer a question of how he writes, just because word and image are for him based on the same evidence and are definitive for him. Instead, you have to look for Dreiser's bad style exactly at those points where he is trying to remedy this nakedness, this expressive realism, and then he contorts and decorates his phrase, in showy ornamental ways which always accompany the digression, the intrusion of the author into the objectivity of the narrative. Indeed, it is impossible to quote a well-written passage by Dreiser, because, since his style is entirely one with the canvas, always huge, of diverse passions minutely recounted in all their "chemism," it would be necessary to quote by chapters. It is much easier instead to give examples of his bad taste, when, especially at the end of the novels, he abandons the exposition of the events, and intrudes the "philosophy" as theory, as *his* interpretation of these events.

> At this cataclysmic moment, and in the face of the utmost, the most urgent need of action, a sudden palsy of the will—of courage—of hate or rage sufficient; and with Roberta from her seat in the stern of the boat gazing at his troubled and then suddenly distorted and fulgurous, yet weak and even unbalanced face—a face of a sudden, instead of angry, ferocious, demoniac—confused and all but meaningless in its registration of a balanced combat between fear (a chemic revulsion against death or murderous brutality that would bring death) and a harried and restless and yet self-repressed desire to do—to do—to do—yet temporarily unbreakable here and now—a static between a powerful compulsion to do and yet not to do.
>
> (*An American Tragedy*)

> Rushing like a great comet to the zenith, his path a blazing trail, Cowperwood did for the hour illuminate the terrors and the wonders of individuality. But for him also the eternal equation—the pathos of the discovery that even giants are but pygmies, and that an ultimate balance must be struck.
>
> (*The Titan*)

Not always, naturally, does bad taste touch these summits; often in *The Financier,* in *The Titan,* and in *The "Genius,"* the digression has only the function of providing a background, and because of its nature is neither in good nor bad taste: it is a question of informative, nonartistic pages. See, for example, in *The Financier,* those interminable passages where a house is furnished or characters are introduced with their entire social curricula. If you then think of those works by Dreiser which are all digression—the reminiscences and the various essays—you find in them, in the more modest tone of the lesser work, a subdued style halfway between the discursive and scientific which, if it won't hold up by comparison with the brawny narrative intensity of the great pages in the major novels, is still far superior to certain baroque flourishes in these latter, stuck in there, it seems, to relieve the reader, almost by parody, from the desolation of other pages.

It is not enough to say that *An American Tragedy* is the best of Dreiser's books because of a narrative rigor that declines every digressive frivolity. That concerns simply the unity of its tone, not its significance. Almost all the material of *An American Tragedy* had already appeared, variously dissociated, in the other novels. Clyde Griffith, the protagonist, son of lay evangelists, early left to himself, without education, full of admiration and of desires for the higher world of wealth and comforts which is personified for him by his millionaire sweetheart Sondra Finchley—"the beautiful Sondra"—has in him, apart from the energy of disposition, much of Cowperwood, or better, of Aileen, who is Cowperwood's first mistress and who follows him, enchanted, into those splendid worlds of his which from one day to the next collapse and are immediately replaced by others. So Roberta Alden—factory worker and Clyde's secret mistress, to free himself from whom, and to run off with Sondra, Clyde finally commits the crime—very much recalls, in her rather stoic sweetness and, later, when she discovers herself pregnant, in the desperate tenacity with which she insists on marriage, the austere femininity of the earlier Sister Carrie. Finally, all the last part of the book—the trial of the murderer Clyde, where the interest is transferred from the protagonists to the defender and to the prosecutor, to a whole court and state, to the mothers of the dead girl and of Clyde, and to punishment itself—is only a rerun, richer, clearer, and more definitive, of an old passion in Dreiser: to conclude a novel with the violent opposition of the protagonist and society, fully armed, all-powerful, and usually victorious. What interests him, in the spectacle of life, is the customary "equilibrium of equations."

But *An American Tragedy* presents especially a reversal of human interest, for which that reader is unprepared who, skimming the other novels, stopped, as is natural, at *The Titan* as the highest point. It seems, before 1925, that Dreiser, partly because of his ideas of the victory of the strongest and partly because of his apparent insensibility as cold observer of the contrasts of life, had objectified his whole ideal in Cowperwood, pirate of the stock market and of the taxpayers, and ever-resurgent Titan. But on the contrary he is of an extremely sensitive and sometimes even childlike nature, who is exalted by the spectacle of "Babel-like" Chicago and who sympathizes, although he theorizes on the law of iron necessity, with the poor worker deprived of art, deprived of thought, deprived of tenderness, an instrument in the hands of indifferent bosses. It is not an accident that America, the mythical country of the self-made man, of the unscrupulous *arriviste,* hasn't yet produced the dionysiac and antisocial exaltation of the superman, as we have seen it here in Europe. This comes about naturally from the state of mind—the transformation of the older Puritan zeal—now widespread in America under the form of social concern, of responsibility, of "service"; consequently, and this has nothing to do with the excellence, or lack of it, of the works, over there the average literary tone is more serious, more persuaded of fulfilling a mission, than it is with us. Of the two most famous, among the many American novelists who have dramatized the captain of industry, Jack London in *Burning Delight* creates a figure who is more an ideal knight than a ruthless superman (his hero literally ends in Arcadia); and Sinclair Lewis in *Dodsworth* examines his tragicomic insufficiencies, his bourgeois and extremely provincial aspirations toward an honored old age. And Dreiser, to the reader who has meditated upon *An American Tragedy,* shows how even the diptych of the Titan was not, after all, the celebration of the strongest, but the simple need to see the bottom of every tragedy, the disconsolate and furious discovery that justice is not of this world, and that not even the efforts of a great individual have any purpose.

In *An American Tragedy,* he does not pass judgment on the case of Clyde Griffith, electrocuted with all the formalities, but he is profoundly enraged with the education which abandons the mind or stifles it with empty precepts; with the society that in its discriminations hatches the germs of the crime; with the judicial establishment that permits the intrusion of extraneous interests into the administration of justice; and even with the prison regime that kills the condemned man a thousand times before abandoning him to the final chair. Not that Dreiser has a ready remedy for all these "injustices." He has not the talent of the thinker, as is proclaimed by his various essays, which run from art to economics, and which furiously repeat commonplaces. He wants to restrict himself to "representing"—and this is an unconscious negation of his pretenses to being a thinker—but his representations plumb the depths of many human actions and express their essential tragedy, and hence their essential pietà. In the light of this pietà it is necessary to follow the story of Roberta Alden, from the first amorous meeting with Clyde, in a canoe on a little lake, to the last outing with her lover on another lake, where he knocks her overboard and drowns her; to follow the story of Clyde's blind aspirations for a world more beautiful, more affluent, and more loving, from the discouraging experiences in a brothel to the misunderstandings with Sondra, "radiant Sondra." But especially it is necessary to read the "insensible" pages in which Clyde, now condemned, waits for months with others in the "death house" for an impossible pardon or for the end, and occasionally for some companion there arrives the summons and the final walk. There is in this group of the condemned something of the victims who wait to be chosen for the sacrifice to a monstrous idol. Because of the solitude in which society keeps them buried and the mechanical coldness with which day by day it disposes of them, it seems like reading the story of individuals already buried. So much so that a curious effect, as of flashes of light in the dark or of shouts heard at a distance in the silence, is made by certain features which still extend toward the world, toward human interest: such as Dreiser's anger at the "idiocy" of having a single wire give light to the cells and current to the electric chair, so that, at every execution, the condemned *feel* from their cells the precise moment of the flash by the dimmed light of the lamps. And I repeat, this tragedy has no moral conclusion, it does not have one and it cannot have one because that isn't in the mind of the author. But the miracle of human pietà revealed in the complex and interminable "equations of emotions" is enough to make it one of the greatest books of these recent times.

INTERPRETATION OF WALT WHITMAN, POET

Too often, it seems to me, the image of Walt Whitman that critics have before their eyes is that of a bearded and venerable old man, busy contemplating a butterfly, or surveying with his meek eyes the ultimate clarity of every joy and sorrow in the universe. Perhaps the fault is that of the photograph, which all definitive editions of *Leaves of Grass* officially issued by Bucke, Harned, and Traubel, the testamentory executors, carry in the frontispiece; perhaps of the myth, created by the enthusiastic disciples, of a majestic prophet who was practically a worker of miracles; or perhaps of unnoticed inertia from the triad that once dominated men's imaginations: Tolstoy–Hugo–Whitman. And yet, as thoroughly as certain works of French and English criticism [1] have destroyed the legend of a prophetic Walt Whitman, grand initiator and

1. It has been also the best, which doesn't mean adequate, criticism of his poetry. Bliss Perry, *Walt Whitman, His Life and Works* (Boston, 1906). Basil De Selincourt, *Walt Whitman, A Critical Study* (London, 1914). Valéry Larbaud, *Étude* (1914), reprinted in *Œuvres choisies de Walt Whitman* (Paris, 1930). H. B. Binns, *Walt Whitman and His Poetry* (London, 1915). Régis Michaud, "Walt Whitman, poète cosmique," in *Mystiques et réalistes anglo-saxons* (Paris, 1918), and "L'expansion poétique" in *Littérature américaine* (Paris, 1928).

founder of new religions, there remains the image of him as a beautiful old man with a white beard, to influence unconsciously the predilections of readers; and by now the opinion is all too widespread [2] that the true, the great Walt is, if not exactly that of the last tired groups of the *Leaves* ("Sands at Seventy," "Good-Bye My Fancy," "Old Age Echoes"), certainly, at least, that of the fleeting impressions of friendship ("Calamus"), of the energetic and tender sketches of war ("Drum-Taps"), and of the fugitive visions in the "Whispers of Heavenly Death." It does seem odd, this rapprochement between a white-bearded Walt Whitman and the "Calamus" poems, written between thirty-five and forty and vibrant with so much youthful vigor and boldness of life. And everybody knows that poetry is neither of youth nor age, it is simply poetry. But indeed I do not speak in this fashion of those groups of the *Leaves* in order to denigrate them: I merely say that Whitman critics, who tend to reduce the entire work *only* to those more direct pages of impressionistic vignette, run the danger of falsifying and terribly diminishing the unique originality of the poet, and, in the end, even of the vignettes. Because in this way the poetry of a fully developed inspiration, which, if it produced the rapid pages of "Calamus," at the same time produced something like the great songs that shine in the first two editions of the *Leaves,* is relegated to the level of the tired and fragmentary garrulity—the judgment is Whitman's own—of an old age that, if I may say so again, was not invariably Olympian.

We forget an all too obvious fact: namely, that the "sage of Camden," giving to the book of his whole life, in the edition of 1881 (the seventh), the form which remained definitive thereafter, was doing nothing more than checking out and concluding, at the age of sixty-two, the results of a work intuited with some clarity at thirty and, at age forty-eight, in the edition of 1867 (the fourth), already for the most part com-

2. For a recent example, cf. Lidia Rho Servi, *Intorno a Walt Whitman* (Turin, 1933).

pleted. And of what Whitman's proud prime of life consisted, during which he meditated and translated into actuality the book, he who has not yet understood it as poetry can get an idea by taking a look at the photograph which is of Walt himself, not yet the "sage of Camden," printed facing the future "Song of Myself" in 1855 in the first edition of the *Leaves*. Here is a giant—dressed in a workman's shirt open at the collar, and with a rough beard—concentrated in two mysterious eyes that, at moments, can even seem tender. I think someone has called it the photograph of a "rowdy." In any case, like it or not, the Walt Whitman of practically all the *Leaves* that count is—for those capable of understanding—this one.

Despite the skeptical attitude that a proper reaction against a rather precritical canonization of the seer has actually fostered, it can be maintained, with good arguments, that Walt Whitman always tallied his work with clear critical awareness. And it figures, besides, since otherwise Walt, a practical man obstinate in the labor of the file, if anyone ever was, has to be made into the antipathetic image of an ecstatic idler into whose ear from time to time a daemon breathed songs. *The Magnificent Idler* is, as a matter of fact, the title of a sprightly fictionalized biography of him written by Cameron Rogers,[3] the scholar who has heretofore, I think, best understood the poet; this is precisely because Rogers has not tried to involve himself in rhetorical discussions of the catalogs or vignettes, of psychic or interior poetry, of pederasty or magnetism, and of all the other eternal Whitmanian trivia, but has firmly recreated his man in gestures, in words, and in situations which every reader can with a little humility glimpse in the poems. And truly Walt Whitman *was* an "idler," in the sense in which every poet is an idler when instead of working he prefers to wander about, turning over in his mind, with great labor and with the rare joys that compensate all such labor,

3. Garden City, New York, 1926.

his lines, or, in an almost biblical sense, his "verses." He was an idler at every ordinary task, because he had other business in hand, that stole from him every interest, and perhaps even a little sleep. But these things have already been said, and very well, by Valéry Larbaud.[4]

What is really important is to hammer home the fact that Walt Whitman knew what he was doing, and that, in brief, like every artist who achieves anything, Walt Whitman pondered his achievement, labored it, lived it, *intended* it, and that, if certain of his theoretical claims seem overstated, according to the lights of our age, demonstrably false or ill-founded, the same thing has happened, or is happening, not only to all artists, but to all men. And if someone, faced with such a sentence as, "Isolated advantages in any rank or grace or fortune—the direct or indirect threads of all the poetry of the past—are in my opinion distasteful to the republican genius, and offer no foundation for its fitting verse," [5] shall observe that these are things not to be said even in jest, it can be retorted that, in the first place, it is precisely through thoughts of this kind that Whitman managed to clarify and define his poetic matter, and that, in the second place, immediately following the heretical sentence, he is pleased to relate an anecdote read in youth, an anecdote that can also serve to remind us how artists, from time immemorial, while theorists were forever discussing genres and schools, knew how to think to some purpose. Rubens was speaking to his pupils, before a painting of uncertain attribution: " 'I do not believe the artist, unknown and perhaps no longer living, who has given the world this legacy, ever belong'd to any school, or ever painted anything but this one picture, which is a personal affair—a piece out of a man's life.' " Recalling these words, at the age of almost seventy, Walt Whitman knew what he was talking about; he knew—better than anyone else in America—what sort of thing a work would be, which was made out of the whole existence of a human being.

4. Larbaud, p. 20.
5. "A Backward Glance O'er Travel'd Roads."

Still, it would be easy, by compiling a list of theoretical passages gathered from the numerous prefaces, explanations, glosses, and reminiscences, which fill the bulk of the *Prose Works,* to throw a paradoxical light on many aspects, among them the most notorious, of the Whitmanian program, and unsuspected consequences would flow from it. Unsuspected not only by the author. As Walt Whitman said: "Our fundamental want to-day in the United States, with closest, amplest reference to present conditions, and to the future, is of a class, and the clear idea of a class, of native authors, literatuses, far higher in grade than any yet known, sacerdotal, modern, fit to cope with our occasions, lands, permeating the whole mass of American mentality, taste, belief, breathing into it a new breath of life . . . affecting politics far more than the popular superficial suffrage, with results inside and underneath the elections of Presidents or Congresses—radiating, begetting appropriate teachers, schools, manners, and, as its grandest result, accomplishing . . . a religious and moral character beneath the political and productive and intellectual bases of the States." Clearly, this is his *idée fixe* and traces of it are to be found everywhere in the *Prose Works.* If we then juxtapose the other, the companion *idée fixe*—no one has yet remarked it in all its full singularity—of world history viewed solely through its supreme literary manifestations, through the great national poems, and if we then remember, according to the confessions of Walt himself, those naturalistic modes of declamation in the open air that scared the sea gulls at Coney Island, or entertained the drivers on the Broadway bus lines at the expense of Homer, Shakespeare, Aeschylus, Ossian, and other immortals, we will find it easy to construct on evidence that paradoxical theory of the phenomenon, Whitman, which has been alluded to. If to the above-mentioned poems—his contemporaries Walter Scott and Alfred Tennyson went, like Ossian, with the great national poets—one adds the prolific journalism of the period, Emerson, works of natural history, compendia of science, melodrama, one will have the entire apparent, external culture of Walt Whitman.

And then, adding up the sum, we can say that Walt Whitman wanted to do for America what the various national poets did in their own time for their own people: Walt Whitman is completely obsessed by this romantic idea which he first transplanted to America, Walt Whitman sees America and the world only as a function of the poem that will express them in the nineteenth century and, in comparison, nothing else matters. It is to his credit—this great primitive, this fierce enemy of any kind of literary life that would detract from the spontaneity of nature—it is to his credit that, for his supreme lament on the exterminated red men, he knew how to say: [6]

> No picture, poem, statement, passing them to the future . . .

Walt Whitman lived so intensely the idea of this mission that, while not saving himself from the obvious failure of such an intention, through it his work was saved from failure. He did not make the primitive poem he dreamed, but the poem of this dream. He did not succeed in the absurdity of creating a poetry appropriate to the democratic and republican world and to the principles of the newly discovered land—because poetry is, after all, one and only one thing—but spending his life repeating in various ways this intention, he made of the intention poetry, the poetry of the discovery of a new world in history and of the singing of it. In brief, to spell out the apparent paradox, he made poetry out of making poetry.

But I have said that Walt Whitman tallied his work with a certain critical acumen. And it might seem from this sample of poetical reasoning that he was not himself clear about the historical importance of his work. The case is complicated. Walt Whitman may have deceived himself about the bearing, the effects, the meaning of the *Leaves;* doubtless, in his intentions he was delirious. But the essence, the nature, of the book is something else again, and I cannot believe that a poet, and especially a poet who, like Walt Whitman, charges himself with

6. "Yonnondio."

the onerous undertaking of renewing the techniques and tones of the age's taste, when he succeeds in producing something essential, is entirely ignorant thereafter how it was done, ignorant, that is to say, for what reason he wrote one way rather than another and one thing rather than another. That goes especially for Walt Whitman, who has not even for defense that equivocal aura of the young poet; but who at thirty years of age, after following various trades, after dreadful attempts at fiction and journalism, put together with great labor, to say the least, in four years, a hundred pages in all, and slowly evolved them, developed them, increased them, tortured them, in a tireless quest. He who thinks of it, even without knowing the work, should find it natural that, with all that secondhand enthusiastic culture, Walt Whitman would come out with programmatic peculiarities. The problem remains that, while the official deans of that culture managed, at best, to squeeze from it only glamorous collections of medieval ballads or hymns to progress, Walt Whitman in reality made out of it—whether because of it or in spite of it—the miracle of *Leaves of Grass.*

And he who knows how to look for them, then finds in the *Prose Works* certain protestations, certain declarations, certain —call them what you will—intuitions, which are clearly among the finest passages in all the confused battleground of Whitman criticism. For example, one observes in the already-mentioned "A Backward Glance O'er Travel'd Roads" the imperturbability with which the poet analyzes the principles and motives of the book. The main thing he says of it is this: ". . . a feeling or ambition to articulate and faithfully express in literary or poetic form, and uncompromisingly, my own physical, emotional, moral, intellectual, and æsthetic Personality, in the midst of, and tallying, the momentous spirit and facts of its immediate days, and of current America—and to exploit that Personality, identified with place and date, in a far more candid and comprehensive sense than any hitherto poem or book." [7] And in the end, after the usual and always foolish ex-

7. "A Backward Glance."

position of the true democratic nature of the *Leaves,* he returns for conclusion to the idea that the book is no expression of an imaginary world, not a gallery of detached illustrations (the vignettes), but a Person, a sensibility, who moves in the real world: " 'Leaves of Grass' indeed (I cannot too often reiterate) has mainly been the outcropping of my own emotional and personal nature—an attempt, from first to last, to put *a Person,* a human being (myself, in the latter half of the Nineteenth Century, in America,) freely, fully and truly on record." That idea, quite apart from its critical application to the works of Walt Whitman, possesses a singular historical importance, because it constitutes the first time anyone in America defined the problem that in the twentieth century every artist in the States once more began to propose for himself. However expressed, the idea is forever fresh, for while a European artist (an ancient) will always maintain that the secret of art is to construct a more or less fictive world, to deny reality in order to put in its place another world, hopefully more significant, a modern American will always tell us that his ambition is entirely to attain to the true nature of things, to see things with virgin eyes, to arrive at that "ultimate grip of reality" [8] which alone is worth recognition. It is a sort of deliberate acclimatizing of oneself in the world and in America. And it is no more than just, then, to acknowledge the fact that Walt Whitman was not only the first to give evidence, with his work, of this tendency in the national cutlure, but that he also discovered it within himself and enunciated it with a greater critical clarity than most of his commentators.

If I do not believe that the *form* of Whitman's poetry consists (as many commentators declare or imply) in an anthology of little scenes outstanding by virtue of their charm, neither do I believe that the architecture of the volume as a

8. The phrase is Sherwood Anderson's in *Dark Laughter,* but the general feeling can be verified only by studying in detail the whole vast field of American literary effort in the last thirty years.

whole has any great efficacy, despite the constant desire of Walt and of his disciples that it should. The brief scenes, or vignettes, are supposed to be fast-moving poems (or parts of poems) of impression, wherein are arrested in their essential lines a person, a place, a thought, a glimpse of landscape. They have, incidentally, the defect that toward old age they came forth all the more frequently and mercilessly, because of the determination—by now both comic and pathetic—of the "sage of Camden" to see in every petty thing signs of his grandiose system, and to express them in a parallel, an image, a description. But in a nature like his, which was always straining toward the prophetic, the vignette, which could also become a little genre piece, was always rather the apologue, the exemplification, justified both by doctrine and by the book. When the most recent critics (quite rightly) denied Whitman's prophetic ambitions, they also in effect removed the basis and the significance of the vignettes, reducing them to wretched fragments, and in the process ruining all discrimination, because naturally, in this climate of bad taste, the sketchiest of the sketches are bound to seem the best: "O Captain! My Captain!" "Come Up from the Fields, Father," and "The Singer in the Prison."

That ultimate justification of the vignettes—namely, the architectural basis of the book of the *Leaves*—represents (anybody can see it) the translation into art of the prophetic impulse, the practical purpose of the book, in the same way as the tortured architecture of the *Divina Commedia.* But whether this architecture of the *Leaves* was made of philosophical material less precious, or whether it less resembles a cathedral, or for whatever reason, I do know that there was less tenacity about it than about that of the *Commedia,* and the most audacious are consequently those who accept it, excusing themselves on the grounds that, in the last analysis, the order of the poetry is, in its essential lines, the chronology of its composition; [9] in which case it is not worth the trouble of

9. Cf. the whole chapter, "Plan," in De Selincourt.

further attention. Not vignettes, then (the tired or humble impressions or the descriptive fragments of the long songs), not construction (the futile hierarchy among pages identical in argument and intensity): where will the form of Whitman be found?

Let us pause over a short epic poem, which is also a very great poem, the most difficult piece in the *Leaves,* the "Song of Myself." This "Song," beginning with the first edition of 1855, stands out in the *Leaves* as the commanding one, although still without a title, and it followed the fortune of the book as a whole, undergoing rearrangements, polishing, deletions, and additions of every kind. In the 1881 edition we find it in definitive shape, fifty-two sections, enormous even among the brood of the early poems "aux titres immenses, les mastodontes et les iguanodons de la création whitmanienne." [10] This "Song of Myself" is something like a quintessence of *Leaves of Grass:* in it all the motives, even when considered as simple subjects, come together. The fascination begins in the fact that, exactly as the entire book has no value as construction, so this poem would manage to sustain without damage huge cuts or huge additions or rearrangements, and besides its author did do this and would still be doing it, were it not for the completely accidental chance of old age and death. Must we then say that the poem's value indubitably resides in the fragmentary little scenes where something realistically defined catches the attention? Not at all, although in it there are negligible pages as well as other pages belonging among the hundred best pages of poetry of all time.

Let's begin with the meter. It is a waste of time, and I've wasted time there myself, minutely going through the *Prose Works* of the good gray poet in the hope of discovering, in *Specimen Days,* among the hospital experiences of the Civil War, or at the happy nudist vacation in the solitudes of Timber Creek, pages, fragments—vignettes, in brief—for comparison with similar motifs in the *Leaves,* for the purpose of dem-

10. Larbaud, p. 32.

onstrating how, ultimately, there is no difference between the verse and the prose. No one admires Whitman's literary prose more than I do, but is it still necessary to remember that nearly all of it was written after the Civil War and during ill health and when his beard was already at least grizzled? I have previously remarked how, from that time on, Walt Whitman tended to revise his poems at length and, although he found the new vein which we might call "contemplative"—cf. all the *Leaves* from "Autumn Rivulets" (1881) to "Old Age Echoes" (posthumous)—still in that Indian summer of impressions, of wise thoughts, of revelatory parallels, of boundless efflorescence, in brief, of vignettes, among many new virtues there is also the lack of that nerve, that shudder, which transfigured even the more allegorical and programmatic pages of the early *Leaves*. Almost all Whitman's poetry from "Autumn Rivulets" (which he commenced writing at the time of the peace of 1865) to his death would gain immensely if it were written in prose, would gain in immediacy, clarity, force; the prose works that accompany and reflect it are, in fact, beyond all argument, preferable. On the contrary, of what he wrote before "Whispers of Heavenly Death" (1871), who searches out, or who today even remembers, the few prose works? There are, thus, two periods in Whitman's career, the first of poetry and the second of prose, and there is a substantial difference between that verse and that prose that one cannot ignore, except by confounding, among other things, what Walt Whitman himself distinguished with so much care.

It may seem superfluous, but is worth repeating, that Walt Whitman, even when he was inventing his poetic line, knew what he was doing. It is not for nothing, in the account he gives of his innovation, or metrical liberation, that he contrasts himself with Poe. The passage reads: "Toward the last I had among much else look'd over Edgar Poe's poems—of which I was not an admirer, tho' I always saw that beyond their limited range of melody (like perpetual chimes of music bells, ringing from lower *b* flat up to *g*) they were melodious expressions, and perhaps never excell'd ones, of certain pronounc'd phases of human morbidity." [11] The slightly ambiguous praise of those effects which, despite their "ringing from lower *b* flat up to *g*" ("like perpetual chimes of music bells"), end in the harmonious expression "of certain pronounc'd phases of human morbidity," proves that Whitman never desired to achieve musicality in sound effects, in "chimes of music bells," but substituted for the traditional schemes his own verse form. And, we can add, wiser by thirty years of experiments, Walt Whitman didn't even dream of writing in our (European) vers libre of the decadence, the exasperation (if anything) precisely of the French and English prodigies of traditional technique achieved in the first half of the century. The nature and range of Whitman's verse are quite other and, as I say, by contrasting himself with the symphonic Poe, Walt Whitman gives evidence of having been entirely aware of the difference.

Walt Whitman had nothing whatever against meter or rhyme for their own sake. He even went so far as to write poems in meter and rhyme. He resented musicality as an end in itself, and this resentment, had he lived to know them, would have made him condemn the vers-librists. His metrical standard, obviously taken from translations of the Bible, does not depend upon phonic laws. Near a verse that runs halfway across the page, we sometimes or often find an extremely long one. Walt Whitman obeys what we might call an imaginative law. He expresses a thought, a click of thought, an image, and then he is off again. He sings through waves of imagination—when the thought within him becomes imaginative—and the harmony spreads from one unit to another unit, clothing and furnishing a voice to the very labor of releasing these visions or thoughts, which are all valuable for themselves and which can burst out in an instant, or over twenty pages that, except for the weariness or the mental encumbrances of the poet,

11. "A Backward Glance."

never reciprocally confuse or cancel each other out. This is the rhythm, created and expressed by the verse, of all the best of the *Leaves,* and it can be readily understood how, having already built in spacious poems all his poetic motifs, and then habituating himself, during and after the war, to a rapid and illustrative form of notation in prose, and henceforth lacking in that ingenuous and splendid joy of the discovery of a world, and of the world, Walt Whitman was transformed, as he grew older, into the subtle contemplator of natural objects, with the involuted impressions and the elderly taste for edifying pictures: things that are all useful—as they were useful to him—more to the skillful prose writer than to the poet who now concerns us.

In order to understand Whitman's best verse, you need only return to "Song of Myself." And the answer to the question, what is the form of his poetry?—not the constructive shape of the ensemble, not the surviving fragments, such as those of his old age—can now be given. The line, the phrase shouted or whispered, the oratorical period—always measured by lines—these are the real form of "Song of Myself" and thus of the *Leaves* as a whole, as long as the author's breath held out.

The opening of "Song of Myself":

> I celebrate myself, and sing myself,
> And what I assume you shall assume,
> For every atom belonging to me as good belongs to you.

and the ending:

> Failing to fetch me at first keep encouraged,
> Missing me one place search another,
> I stop somewhere waiting for you.

that could so easily be exchanged without apparent damage, although between them there is displayed every kind of poetic inspiration, all equally interchangeable: those two excerpts are not beautiful because they introduce or conclude a particular vision, or because they expound or help to construct any such vision, but they are valuable in their own right, for their eloquent flow, where every line is a complete whole, with its own harmonies and its own significance. It could be said that Walt Whitman thinks in lines, that is to say, that with him every thought, every flash of inspiration, creates for itself a definitive form in which it consists, and does not lapse into a rhythm preexistent or subject to other laws. The highs and lows of Whitman's "music" are the highs and lows of his imaginative state. And therefore they are not fragments: it is no longer fragmentary, a poetry that simplifies itself to the point of revealing itself founded and created by the line, by the end-stop of every metrical unit. "I celebrate myself, and sing myself" is not a fragment. It is the definition, repeated and varied by Walt Whitman in a thousand ways, of his discovery of how delightful and magnificent is the simple fact of life.

> Walt Whitman, a kosmos, of Manhattan the son . . .
> Now I will do nothing but listen . . .
> Alone far in the wilds and mountains I hunt . . .
> I am of old and young, of the foolish as much as the wise . . .
> I am the poet of the Body and I am the poet of the Soul . . .

are so many opening lines in sections of "Song of Myself." In each case what follows, instead of developing a suggested motif, repeats, in different details and in different shades of thought, the initial attitude of a man who is endlessly affirming how wonderful it is to discover and embrace the whole of life. Naturally, in the process of illustration, the idea is somewhat strained: sometimes the image demands of Whitman several lines, sometimes one thought is logically tied to another, but there remains the incontrovertible fact of the vigorous affirmation of each line, complete, uttered as if it were the epitome of the entire book and at the same time the most ingenuous and novel and fresh detail of the section. But this phenomenon is explicable only in terms of the nature of those Whitmanian thoughts and visions which inform the lines.

The immense "Song of Myself," whose fifty-two sections I wouldn't swear all the critics have read all the way through, is truly their touchstone. Between a critic who says that " 'Song of Myself' is perhaps not a poem at all. But it is one of the most astonishing expressions of vital energy ever got into a book" [12] and another who implies that it is a kind of Sermon on the Mount ("Such is the song which was sung by the Prophet of the New Era on the Mount of Vision"),[13] the second is not necessarily the more deluded. Certainly, "Song of Myself" contains in its sheer size and in its modes the whole quintessence of the Whitmanian vices and virtues. So bizarre is the mode of the poem that one is almost tempted to believe Walt Whitman, or, worse, the critic, and look here for a poetry of an altogether new sort: not a short epic poem but "an expression of vital energy." But this is just human weakness. A moment's consideration convinces us that even "Song of Myself," the "*tremendous* 'Song of Myself,' " [14] cannot possibly be, through any conceivable eccentricity, anything else but lyric poetry—whether or not a success is the job set for critical inquiry—in brief, the expression of a state of soul, not more nor less than the poetry of, say, Keats, with whom Whitman critics so delight in contrasting Walt Whitman.[15] It is still the tale of Ariosto and Dante: one must be the artist and the other the poet.

I have said repeatedly that the poem has no structure, no plot, to make the parts necessary to the construction. To summarize the poem is not at all easy and it would signify nothing. It must be noted that every other major poem by Walt Whitman (for example, "The Mystic Trumpeter" or "Out of the Cradle Endlessly Rocking") reveals, upon close examination, how its value, its life, consists in something more

12. John Bailey, *Walt Whitman* (New York, 1926), p. 146.
13. Will Hayes, *Walt Whitman, The Prophet of the New Era* (London, 1921), p. 37.
14. Bailey, p. 21.
15. Perry, the last pages of ch. 6; James Thompson, *Walt Whitman, the Man and the Poet* (London, 1910), ch. 1.

profound, in a spirit at once more immediate and more impalpable, than the casual logical or narrative design. Or, if you want to put the matter differently, all Whitman's great pages (I mean those which alone concern us here, those written before Walt Whitman's art developed into a prose, strong and ordered even in its impressionism), all the poems of the prime of life always take the same pattern: the strong, thoughtful, "receptive" man who passes among the phenomena of the world and absorbs them all, enraptured just by their simplicity, their normality, their reality, and who responds to them with an affection, a perpetual ecstacy, born from the imaginative identification of the man with men and things.

On this point Walt Whitman is still, as usual, his own best critic:

> Beginning my studies the first step pleas'd me so much,
> The mere fact consciousness, these forms, the power of motion,
> The least insect or animal, the senses, eyesight, love,
> The first step I say awed me and pleas'd me so much,
> I have hardly gone and hardly wish'd to go any farther,
> But stop and loiter all the time to sing it in ecstatic songs.

So interpreted, even "Song of Myself" reveals itself. That delicate structure—the ego which proclaims its own independence (sections 1–8), is annihilated in the face of experiences (9–19), then reappears in flesh and spirit (20–24), and finally, after another chaos of experiences (25–45), in a manly way embraces the Thou, the perfect Companion (46–52)—appears to be the typical Whitmanian structure: no people, no events, except as details of an immense field of experiences, the universe, and only one person, only one event, which embraces and absorbs everything, the "Myself," the "Comrade," the cataloger—through himself—of the whole universe.

These principles established, to reread most of the Whitman criticism turns out to be entertaining in the extreme, for example, the kind that discusses whether the "Calamus" group is really poetry of friendship ("love without sex") or whether the group preceding it, "Children of Adam," is really erotic poetry ("sex without love").[16] All this confusion excites indignations and defenses and biographical disquisitions turning on the suspicion of homosexuality, which, among other things, because of the restraints and unsubtle innuendoes of the heavy-handed literati of Puritan descent, becomes a damn nuisance to penetrate and follow.[17]

Consider, for example, one of the "libertine" poems from "Children of Adam":

NATIVE MOMENTS

Native moments—when you come upon me—ah you are here now,
Give me now libidinous joys only,
Give me the drench of my passions, give me life coarse and rank,
To-day I go consort with Nature's darlings, to-night too,
I am for those who believe in loose delights, I share the midnight orgies of young men,
I dance with the dancers and drink with the drinkers,
The echoes ring with our indecent calls, I pick out some low person for my dearest friend,
He shall be lawless, rude, illiterate, he shall be one condemn'd by others for deeds done,
I will play a part no longer, why should I exile myself from my companions?
O you shunn'd persons, I at least do not shun you,
I come forthwith in your midst, I will be your poet,
I will be more to you than to any of the rest.

Anyone can see, after a light polemical coloration is stripped away, that the poem represents a moment in the usual Whitmanian passion: to confront one experience out of

16. De Selincourt, pp. 207–208.
17. Is it so difficult to express ourselves with the scientific clarity of J. Schlaf who, clear as the sun, entitled his study, *Walt Whitman, Homosexual?* In this connection, one must go read Perry's pages in the chapter, "The Caresser of Life" (pp. 44–48) where, discussing the famous letter from J. A. Symonds and the reply by Walt Whitman (10 August 1890), the moral character of the latter is defended with so many apparent reticences that, through a legitimate impatience, we practically want to believe the contrary.

thousands, and to lose oneself, to merge oneself in it—poetry of discovery. Anyone can see that the "shunn'd persons" are no other than the usual "Comrade," the usual Whitmanian alter ego, subsuming, from time to time, the whole universe. But even De Selincourt, who elsewhere shows himself anything but stupid, prefers subtly to demonstrate that Walt Whitman never had the shameful experiences enumerated in "Native Moments," for the simple reason that, precisely because these experiences are longed for and invoked, their poet could not have been through them.[18]

This confusion of biographical and aesthetic problems has raged around the two "amorous" groups of the Leaves, beclouding many an otherwise clear perception. Whereas, to unclouded eyes, the truth is that "Children of Adam" and "Calamus" are the same old hymn to the perfect Whitmanian individual—woman or man, it makes no difference—who experiences the joy, the health, the freedom of every contact with the objects of the universe, leaves of grass, another body, a "prophetic" thought. Walt Whitman can't be understood at all until we realize that the various personæ, which are empirically imposed on his song at various moments in his existence, are only a single figure, identified (and their life consists in this identification) from time to time with various areas of experience. Thus the lovers and the friends (or, better, the comrades) of the two "amorous" groups; thus the soldiers (or, better, the comrades) of the Civil War; thus the pioneers (or, better, the comrades) of the great songs about America, and of whom the figure of Lincoln is typical; thus even the otherworldly appearances, the celestial presences (or, better, the comrades) of "Whispers of Heavenly Death."

In the first groups, it is significant how indifferently Walt Whitman names the body of women next to that of men. Let's forget the offended conscience; it is quite irrelevant, since there never passed through Walt Whitman's mind a thought

18. De Selincourt, pp. 26–28.

lascivious in itself, but rather there sprang to his lips cries of gratitude for the inexhaustible field of experiences, of discoveries, of identifications; in any case, beyond man and woman, there are even the fields of earth and of sea and finally of the whole receiving universe:

> Arms and hands of love, lips of love, phallic thumb of love,
> breasts of love, bellies press'd and glued together with
> love,
> Earth of chaste love, life that is only life after love,
> The body of my love, the body of the woman I love, the
> body of the man, the body of the earth,
> Soft forenoon airs that blow from the south-west . . .

So he goes on, invoking the murmur of bees, the smell of apples, the sweats of his body, his Adamic daughters, in short, all the symphonic material of his least erotic pages, and the whole performance floats in the same early morning atmosphere of joy toward things which tenderly and for the first time disclose themselves.

Consider how little of the usual eros, and how much "comradeship" instead, there is in his women:

> They are not one jot less than I am,
> They are tann'd in the face by shining suns and blowing
> winds,
> Their flesh has the old divine suppleness and strength,
> They know how to swim, row, ride, wrestle, shoot, run,
> strike, retreat, advance, resist, defend themselves.

Consider the perfect identification, the perfect "comradeship," the same which concludes with an embrace all the long songs of discovery, here isolated in a new kind of lyric:

> O you whom I often and silently come where you are that I
> may be with you,
> As I walk by your side or sit near, or remain in the same
> room with you,
> Little you know the subtle electric fire that for your sake is
> playing within me.

The same goes for Whitman's soldiers. They are neither the epic heroes of a *chanson de geste* nor the reluctant doughboys of the World War. They are the "comrades" who, in the more programmatic moments, struggle to save the democratic Union, and, in the more poetic moments, share with Walt Whitman the experiences, the emotions, the energetic discovery of other human beings:

> The crush'd head I dress, (poor crazed hand tear not the
> bandage away,)
> The neck of the cavalry-man with the bullet through and
> through I examine,
> Hard the breathing rattles, quite glazed already the eye, yet
> life struggles hard,
> (Come sweet death! be persuaded O beautiful death!
> In mercy come quickly.)

The same with the "whispers of heavenly death," where even out of death Walt Whitman manages to create a myth of discovery, an ecstatic voyage among otherworldly glimmerings, intuitions, frissons, a confident anticipation of the embrace of a divine "comrade" who awaits and who will treat the arrival as an equal, as befits the pioneer who treated the entire universe this way, from a drop of water to a star.

> Darest thou now O soul,
> Walk out with me toward the unknown region,
> Where neither ground is for the feet nor any path to follow?
>
> No map there, nor guide,
> Nor voice sounding, nor touch of human hand,
> Nor face with blooming flesh, nor lips, nor eyes, are in that
> land.
>
> I know it not O soul,
> Nor dost thou, all is a blank before us,
> All waits undream'd of in that region, that inaccessible
> land.
>
> Till when the ties loosen,
> All but the ties eternal, Time and Space,

Nor darkness, gravitation, sense, nor any bounds bounding
us.

Then we burst forth, we float,
In Time and Space O soul, prepared for them,
Equal, equipt at last, (O joy! O fruit of all!) them to fulfill
O soul.

Walt Whitman is the poet of this discovery, whether it be the discovery of a blade of grass, or of President Lincoln, or, in the moments of a vein less pure, less ours, of the American Union. It is through his cosmic wonder over things and people that Walt Whitman gives life to the dessicated romantic intention of making the primitive poem of America. He never sings America: he sings himself intent on discovering America as—and it is here that he is most turbid—a political entity; but he also sings himself absorbed in the discovery of a life of which America is only an atom, or, in the least happy moments, artistically speaking, a symbol.

All this tends to make Walt Whitman essentially a cataloger. This problem of the catalogs is second in importance, among critics, only to the other question, whether or not Whitman wrote metrically. And, in passing, it should be noted how the critical contrivance of the vignettes, of the fragments, had and still has the effect of relegating to a limbo of the uncreated all Whitman's catalog pages. Now, we may grant that many of the vignettes of the elder Whitman are not altogether tired, not altogether self-parodic, but only in the light of the recognition that they are still pallid echoes of those proud lists of quite rapid and clearly defined vignettes which were the catalogs of the great songs.

"Song of Myself" is full of them:

The little one sleeps in its cradle,
I lift the gauze and look a long time, and silently brush
away flies with my hand.

The youngster and the red-faced girl turn aside up the busy
hill,

I peeringly view them from the top.
The suicide sprawls on the bloody floor of the bedroom . . .
The pure contralto sings in the organ loft,
The carpenter dresses his plank, the tongue of his foreplane whistles its wild ascending lisp . . .

Except in some cases where a political statement intrudes, whether practical or bravura, all Whitman's catalog poems belong among his best, as is obvious from an absolutely convincing example in "Our Old Feuillage":

On rivers boatmen safely moor'd at nightfall in their boats under shelter of high banks,
Some of the younger men dance to the sound of the banjo or fiddle, others sit on the gunwale smoking and talking;
Late in the afternoon the mocking-bird, the American mimic, singing in the Great Dismal Swamp,
There are the greenish waters, the resinous odor, the plenteous moss, the cypress-tree, and the juniper-tree;
Northward, young men of Mannahatta, the target company from an excursion returning home at evening, the musket-muzzles all bear bunches of flowers presented by women.

And besides, when in many of the short poems (as in "Calamus," in "Drum-Taps," and in "Whispers of Heavenly Death") Walt Whitman so often resorts to another material, more logical and more constructive, it is always a question of a technical foreshortening through which a rational explanation, or the setting of a clearly defined scene, frames the usual instant of ecstasy, of loving and essential contact with a comrade, a synthetic universal "Thou," whether a person or a thing.

So much is evident also in the conclusion of "Song of Myself," where there is no longer a catalog of experiences with which the "myself" identifies itself, but a tremulous atmosphere of miracle come to pass is spread before the vision-laden eyes of the reader:

50

There is that in me—I do not know what it is—but I know it is in me.
Wrench'd and sweaty—calm and cool then my body becomes,
I sleep—I sleep long.
I do not know it—it is without name—it is a word unsaid,
It is not in any dictionary, utterance, symbol.
Something it swings on more than the earth I swing on,
To it the creation is the friend whose embracing awakes me.

Perhaps I might tell more. Outlines! I plead for my brothers and sisters.
Do you see O my brothers and sisters?
It is not chaos or death—it is form, union, plan—it is eternal life—it is Happiness.

51

The past and present wilt—I have fill'd them, emptied them,
And proceed to fill my next fold of the future.
Listener up there! what have you to confide to me?
Look in my face while I snuff the sidle of evening,
(Talk honestly, no one else hears you, and I stay only a minute longer.)
Do I contradict myself?
Very well then I contradict myself,
(I am large, I contain multitudes.)

I concentrate toward them that are nigh, I wait on the door-slab.
Who has done his day's work? who will soonest be through with his supper?
Who wishes to walk with me?
Will you speak before I am gone? will you prove already too late?

52

The spotted hawk swoops by and accuses me, he complains of my gab and my loitering.
I too am not a bit tamed, I too am untranslatable,
I sound my barbaric yawp over the roofs of the world.
The last scud of day holds back for me,
It flings my likeness after the rest and true as any on the shadow'd wilds,

It coaxes me to the vapor and the dusk.
I depart as air, I shake my white locks at the runaway sun,
I effuse my flesh in eddies, and drift it in lacy jags.
I bequeath myself to the dirt to grow from the grass I love,
If you want me again look for me under your boot-soles.
You will hardly know who I am or what I mean,
But I shall be good health to you nevertheless,
And filter and fibre your blood.
Failing to fetch me at first keep encouraged,
Missing me one place search another,
I stop somewhere waiting for you.

Anyone can now see how Walt Whitman's poetry works: it consists of successive thoughts, all exploding from the plenitude that the identification with all things experienced begets in the "myself." It is the joy of the successive discovery of these thoughts, and thus their dynamic importance, not their logical value, that matters:

Do I contradict myself?
Very well then I contradict myself,
(I am large, I contain multitudes.)

Every thought is really thought on the instant, the verse made of the daring and diversity of the mind in action, which beholds itself in the act of thinking the thought, and expresses its consciousness of it. Walt Whitman sings the joy of discovering thoughts.

And another thing is apparent here. The hawk, which appears in the final section, is not an image, or at least not in the direct way in which we understand the term image. It is one of the many presences of the universe with which Walt Whitman identifies himself. It is a detail from a catalog. Images don't exist for Walt Whitman, and he who recalls the "nest of guarded duplicate eggs" and the belt stringing the huge oval lakes—to hold up the States' pants, I suppose—will of course be convinced of it. Walt Whitman tends to experience in language a simple clarity and an unmediated response to things, of a primal flavor, and is so much the more himself when he expresses his object directly. Moreover, what in another poet would become an excuse for a whole shower of images, becomes in him an interior landscape, infinite and always renewed, which of the two ends of comparison makes two rapid moments of the same vision or discovery.

It is no use, then, to object [19] that certain lists of mere names, such as geographical names in "Salut au Monde" or anatomical details in "I Sing the Body Electric"—

> Head, neck, hair, ears, drop and tympan of the ears,
> Eyes, eye-fringes, iris of the eye, eyebrows, and the waking or sleeping of the lids,
> Mouth, tongue, lips, teeth, roof of the mouth, jaws, and the jaw-hinges,
> Nose, nostrils of the nose, and the partition,
> Cheeks, temples, forehead, chin, throat, back of the neck, neck-slue,
> Strong shoulders, manly beard, scapula, hind-shoulders, and the ample side-round of the chest—

it is no use to object that these things are the evidence of the bad services that the deprecated technique of the early poems rendered to Walt Whitman. Obviously, when catalogs are composed with the dictionary or encyclopedia at hand, simply to fill out a predetermined argument, no poetry results. But this fact does not refute, indeed it corroborates, as psychological proof, the hypothesis that the true nature of Walt Whitman is precisely in his not being satisfied with a little scene, a perfected vignette, for its own sake, but with the expression—and in his weak moments with the invocation—of the desire and the yearning and the ever-resurgent pleasure of feeling the whole surrounding universe as a presence brotherly and real.

19. Carleton Noyes, *An Approach to Walt Whitman* (Boston, 1910), the chapter entitled "Walt Whitman's Art." But all the Whitman scholars are irritated with the catalogs, except for De Selincourt who excogitates in their defense the following theory: the catalogs are the truest technique of the Whitmanian poetical imagination, because in them the dead parts (mere names), side by side with the living (little scenes more enriched with details), come together in a song of universality, that is, they present, in their opposition, all the good and all the evil of the world. Nevertheless, this eccentricity is meritorious, especially if taken with all the rest of the chapter (on "Style") where, through many freaks and obscurities, there suddenly issues: "his poetry is his desire for poetry" (p. 139).

FAULKNER, A BAD PUPIL OF ANDERSON

Faulkner's novel *Sanctuary* (1931), which is in the process of becoming fashionable, even here, through the French version and the film *Perdizione,* takes place in the states of Mississippi and Tennessee, first in an abandoned, ruined plantation house where bootleggers manufacture whiskey and live together rather communally, and later at Memphis and Jefferson, now in a whorehouse, now in prison. We are told of an eighteen-year old college girl raped with a corncob by an impotent bootlegger; of the arrest and trial of a ring-leader innocent of the rape; of the lynching (corncobs and gasoline) of the latter by the mob; and of the legal hanging of the unsuspected rapist for the mere killing of a policeman. Temple—the college girl—raped, as aforesaid, by the impotent Popeye, at the plantation house where she happened to come with Gowan, a drunken student, is carried off to Memphis, to Miss Reba's whorehouse, where she lives locked up and where Popeye comes to visit and enjoy her by means of Red, a young hood, who in his presence plays the role that Popeye cannot play. Then we have prison and court for the ring-leader, Goodwin, a man inexplicably noble, accused of a murder committed by Popeye and, later, of the rape. Amidst threats and cold treatment, the absentminded lawyer, Horace Benbow, undertakes a defense which has no clear result; in any case, Goodwin is lynched by a mob, with all the observances of appropriate retaliation. Popeye, of whom we have meanwhile learned that since he was a child he has been characterized by bloodthirsty insanity (he used to cut live birds and cats in two with scissors), is uselessly hanged for a trivial murder. There are not lacking glimpses of various backgrounds: the novel rather aspires to render the whole atmosphere of the Southern states. We have a suggestion of politics (campaign corruption), several domestic interiors (narrow-minded gossips), a gangster funeral (cynicism), a little obscure adolescent psychology (the two teen-age boys who take rooms in the Memphis whorehouse, as at a *pensione,* and don't notice the difference), and finally a Negro condemned to death for murder, who sings spirituals.

I say all this, not lightly to destroy the novel as a document of morbid defeatist fantasies which threatens the delicate balance of the Latin reader, or whatever, but to define the tone of its pages, which would appear, from what we have seen, to be one of bitter moral disillusion, of a stunted and disheartening Puritanism which tortures itself with the tragic contrast between bestiality and human justice, equally blind and impotent.

It so happens, however, that, as someone said without I think weighing the importance of the expression, William Faulkner "writes like an angel"—I mean, with the detachment and the projection of events in a rarefied atmosphere that would be legitimate in a pure spirit. In so many pages of perversions, of morbid perplexities, of obscene and bloody cirmes, there is not one single concession to lust, which would be a lesser evil, or even to moral indignation or to cynical pleasure. William Faulkner sees things from on high, from so high that between Popeye's bloody corncob and Benbow's forgotten pipe there is no difference in levels. It is not a man who writes, but an angel, an angel, of course, without a cure of souls.

Therefore, the book must be absolved of any suspicion of Puritan moralizing. William Faulkner is not—or at least he is not here—either the national champion of sanitized morality or the subverter (also Puritan) of national moralistic concepts, which almost all the American rebels have been for thirty years.

There is in the novel one character, and only one, who nods in the direction of moralizing, of somehow bringing into the midst of the action the evaluating personality of the author: Horace Benbow, the lawyer. He, having witnessed some of the plantation house prologue and having come to know there Goodwin's woman, a female strangely soft-spoken and strong, partly through attachment to the woman, partly through love of justice, has undertaken Goodwin's defense; and for the whole time, this Benbow meditates, imagines, investigates, gets himself involved with all kinds of characters, revealing a certain kind of inner life that evaluates—man confused and absentminded—which is as disordered and banal as anything invented by the author.

In this kind of protagonist, we can more easily recognize the influence William Faulkner has undergone from Sherwood Anderson. The real meat of Anderson is the South and bewildered characters who are always analyzing themselves; and it is surely necessary to recognize a common fund of suggestions and sympathies in the two writers. To remind ourselves how in Anderson every character is made up of introspective material, is in one way or another perplexed, analyzes himself and tells his own story to himself, clarifies the nature of Faulkner, who up to a certain point preserves the same abstracted tone of unceasing wonder, of slow reality, which Anderson obtains in his characters with the teeming of an inner life never interrupted and always imaginatively coherent. But the abstracted tone, the "slow reality" of Faulkner, is not born of a narrative labor intrinsic to each character or even of a skillful imaginative introspection (there come to mind the flat and wearisome "interior monologues" of *As I Lay Dying,* written a year before *Sanctuary*): Faulkner has simply preserved Anderson's technique of throwing a spell of wonder over certain details of everyday life; of making a voice, a conversation, explode in the midst of a highly charged silence, resulting in a tension almost miraculous; of creating an aura around his characters by means of the rhythmical repetition of certain actions or distinguishing features. Faulkner's "slow motion" lacks that "something to say" which would justify it, that which in each of Anderson's characters is the pleasure, the imaginative need, of seeing himself in action, of telling himself. Actually, we are seldom bored in reading Anderson, or at any rate we seldom notice the slowness of the style; in Faulkner we continually feel that anguish, that nearly physical constriction which we feel watching a film in slow motion. The entire adventure of Temple in the plantation house—the first half of the book—is the most notable example of this asthmatic style. Popeye reveals even better the exteriority of this transfiguring technique: at the end of the action, after the "monster" has perpetrated all his evil in the "angelic" atmosphere of rarefication which we have seen, the author must have recourse to a chronicle-style exposition of a clinical case—the monstrous childhood and youth of the hero—that alone can furnish the key to the events recounted. Which observation can even justify us in defining *Sanctuary*, with well-deserved severity, as a too ambitious thriller.

THE FICTIONALIZED BIOGRAPHIES OF SINCLAIR LEWIS

Since he was awarded the Nobel prize Sinclair Lewis has written at least two other novels: *Ann Vickers* and *Work of Art*. Meanwhile, the documentary nature of his work becomes ever more clear. Episodes such as Ann Vickers' experience in the penitentiary are mere chronicle, colored by a very lively style, but still chronicle, a juxtaposition of facts, in short, document. Someone [1] has said that of the older American literary generation which flourished from 1910 to 1915, it is Lee Masters, O'Neill, Anderson, etc., with their psychoanalytical introspections, their "clinical cases," who are the documentaries, the stillbirths, whereas Lewis alone had begun to express in his novels that more genial and smiling and human view of the world which everybody, and especially his compatriots, was waiting for. This formula demands closer examination, this formula with which people want to get rid of the "psychoanalytics," of whom it can never be too often said that —even if sometimes somebody, through a mistaken cultural preoccupation, delights to pose, in the realm of poetry, as a scientific investigator of previously unexplored experiences—still

1. Beniamino de Ritis, "Mente puritana in corpo pagano," *Nuova Antologia,* 16 February 1934.

the best of their works are made up of rich human pages, where quite often the critic has to work hard decently to understand and to value new expressive means and new poetical worlds, rather than to look down his nose under some pretext.

As for Lewis, it is cruel, or worse, to make him stand for all that little stock of good which hardworking twentieth-century America is supposed to have produced in the field of poetry. Those of us who in our day turned many of Lewis' pages, even lovingly, are now more than ever convinced that this writer's interest lay rather in the "matter" of his books than in that artistic workmanship which some people would like to impute to them. All the elements of his work refer to a cultural and social world which has not yet ceased to interest us, although the surprise of its novelty is past; but everything, from the train of events to the language ascribed to the characters, interests us in its materiality: the events as representative chronicle, the language as philological document.

It seems to me generally accepted now that it is a completely false opinion that makes Lewis the simple satirist of his society, the satisfied creator of representative ridiculous puppets; anyone who, having read *Babbitt* carelessly, still thinks this, can look at *Arrowsmith* and *Ann Vickers* especially, where the compassionate and youthfully enthusiastic soul of the author is completely—and indeed too much—revealed. What happened to Mark Twain is happening to Lewis: having got off four epigrams against America, all their work has risked passing for a persistent satire of the people and things of the nation. But, unlike Mark Twain who, for example, in the adventures of the two runaways on the Mississippi (*The Adventures of Huckleberry Finn*), undeniably touched the chords of real poetry—not to mention the creation of a language of his own, of great originality in the stylistic tradition of America, nourished by many dialects from the river valleys —Lewis, although he actually goes beyond satire, lacks that power of transfiguration, of restoring the virginal freshness of reality, which can make something definitive even of a pun. It is necessary to recognize, renouncing the attractive notion that Lewis marks a step forward in the creation of an autochthonous linguistic medium, that slang and the vernacular remain in him local color, not yet stripped of their corporeality. This is confirmed by the fact that his linguistic fireworks are limited to dialogue, and that the style of the narrative proper doesn't escape from the slightly flat generality of journalistic jargon. To write the true story of the native American language, you would have to linger over such names as Walt Whitman, Mark Twain, O. Henry, Sherwood Anderson, and John Dos Passos.

Lewis' characters have all the external complication and internal monotony of the heroes in the local news. Sarcastically he prefaces *Elmer Gantry* with the remark: "No character in this book is the portrait of any actual person." The point is instead precisely this: Lewis' characters *are* "actual persons," so "actual," that is to say, ordinary, conventional, "men in the street," that their hatreds and passions do not go beyond the summary notation of the daily news; so much "persons" that Lewis does not know how to caricature them freely and make of them a world coherently deformed, a grotesque fantasy that is self-sufficient. In this connection, it is useful to notice the technical construction of these novels: the germ, the pretext, seems to me always to be external. With proper complications, of course. *Main Street* is entirely worked up from the setting of a small provincial town; *Babbitt* from the world of the businessman; *Arrowsmith* from that of doctors; *Elmer Gantry* from that of religionists; *Dodsworth* from the big industrialists; *Ann Vickers* from prisons. There is something mechanical —virtuoso and amateurish at once—in all this: Lewis decides on a background, a profession, and out it comes. By those who want to be malicious, these gadget novels could be called biographies à la Ludwig: the literary jack-of-all-trades selects his subjects as he goes along for purely extrinsic reasons (the celebrity of a name, the importance of a profession), and from this choice his reconstructions follow. In fact, the real characters in Lewis are backgrounds and professions, and the people are only imitations. Certainly, in this sense Lewis is a romancer, since in life we find people just like his characters—but only in America, so "actual" are they—whereas no one will ever meet in life a character from great poetry, not even if he runs into the poet.

Once this limitation is imposed on the novelist, it is not worth the trouble to insist on the scheme that reveals the intimately mechanical nature of the invention. It is evident that Lewis' heroes all live the same adventure of suffocation, restlessness, and return to themselves: an ironic alternation of flights and imprisonments. That much established, it is useless to comment on the inventive poverty of the author, who can presumably only alter the external circumstances (the world of science, the world of business, the world of art, etc.), repeating unchanged the formal and psychological shape of the action. It is more profitable, instead, to settle for, and to search out, that which in him, after all, deserves to be enjoyed: the spectacle of a mutable and many-colored reality, full of evidences of a life lived with much, even with too much, enthusiasm.

Part Two: 1938–1950

PREFACE TO THE AUTOBIOGRAPHY OF ALICE B. TOKLAS

That this *Autobiography* was written, not by the protagonist, but by one of the characters, is something more than a trick: it is the signature of a whole style. Some readers will think themselves faced with a simple collection of anecdotes, others with a re-creation of milieux, still others with an attempt to relate an unusual intellectual formation. It is characteristic of living works thus to present themselves many-faceted and diverse. The *Autobiography* indubitably contains a collection of anecdotes so unlikely that they must be true and a gallery of milieux so true that they would seem invented. And it follows the story of several intellectual developments with so much sympathy that even the gossip about bibliographical details receives life from it. But this is not yet the book. The anecdotes, the milieux, and the people play their part in a vaster and richer game, exactly that which the sly joke of the conclusion implies: "About six weeks ago Gertrude Stein said, it does not look to me as if you were ever going to write that autobiography. You know what I am going to do. I am going to write it for you."

The worst judgment that you could give of this work would be to declare that this conclusion is unexpected. To me it seems rather the gay signature on the canvas, so subtly does the mystifying smile illuminate the text from top to bottom. Nor can this attitude of the author be called monotonous. See how malicious the smile becomes when "Alice Toklas" judges herself severely, and how anxious instead when the most devilish opinions are delivered to Gertrude Stein on the work of Gertrude Stein. Exactly in this game of mirrors—Gertrude Stein who talks about Gertrude Stein through the mouth of the garrulous Alice Toklas—consists the rich secret of this prose. On all that Gertrude Stein says and does there has descended a wonderful ambiguity, which detaches, lightens, and renders ironic her words and her actions, in the same way that, looking at ourselves in a mirror, it happens to all of us to feel ourselves different and irresponsible. Not even when third persons appear on the scene does the smiling atmosphere chill, because Gertrude Stein's glance retains through the whole book the capacity of turning, amused and curious, upon each other person as upon herself. This tone, finally—and this is the proof of a fundamental sincerity—renders so much more convincing those solemn and affirmative declarations which constitute the professions of poetical faith of the author or of some kindred spirit.

If it were possible here to retell—after all the words that Gertrude Stein has expended in this book—her thirty years of literary labors and to list the works, there would be plainly revealed the reasons not only why I have chosen to introduce into Italy of all her books this one, but also why I think that in it Gertrude Stein has said her finest word. For in brief the tireless experimenter of the hermetic portraits and of the rhythmic oceanic measured sentences has here finally achieved the contemplation, ironic and at the same time compassionate, of a real world, apart from any too complacent interest in the procedures of art. Others—and she herself, perhaps—will speak of the importance which those experiments and those investigations had for the literary renaissance (not only American) of the postwar period; and they will be able to retrace her precursors in the figures of Walt Whitman or Henry James—of Walt Whitman especially, to whom she is the perhaps unconfessed debtor for that wholly American idea of a mystic reality incarnated and imprisoned in the word, that disturbing realism of the subconscious life which is still, down to the present moment, the most vital contribution of America to culture. For me, this little book doesn't warrant so complex a lecture, which additionally would seem to me to offend in this way its smiling delicacy.

And a similar scruple of discretion suggests that I would do a pedantic and ill-bred thing if I should be induced to preface here vague remarks on the exceptional milieu of artists and writers that the *Autobiography* evokes. Where the name of a painter, of a poet, or of an eccentric fails to take shape for the reader in a face, a phrase, in a simple gesture, it is indeed useless for a note or a foreword to furnish information about it. But it is very infrequently that the names of the *Autobiography* remain mere names. And the author's concern, even in the most sophisticated context, is so genuinely human that no material information can, in my opinion, add anything to the evidence of the text.

PREFACE TO "BENITO CERENO"

This novella, which appeared for the first time in 1855, and was included the year after in *The Piazza Tales,* is one of the last creative flashes attempted by the imagination of Herman Melville. The prodigious decade (1845–1855), which saw the publication, one year after another, of nearly all his works, was rounding to a close. After 1857 Melville will enter his long silence which, hardly ruffled by a tired poetical effort that the author would be the last to believe in, will persist until death, which occurred at the age of seventy-two in 1891. An exception, the novella *Billy Budd,* composed a few months before the end, is a happy incongruity, a fruit out of season.

One by one Melville's most ambitious works—*Mardi, Moby-Dick, Pierre*—had fallen into a lake of indifference, exciting at the most some contemptuous and savage criticisms, and dissipating that early climate of curiosity which had surrounded the protagonist of the Polynesian adventures, the "man who lived among the cannibals." The pregnant richness of his new style, and of the worlds evoked by him, where the tendency to leave the beaten path of the sensible in order to get lost in the forest of correspondences and of symbols was always more accentuated, disturbed and offended a public much more provincial and Victorian than its contemporary British counterpart. The more Melville strove to bring to light and to transfigure in spiritual symbols his exotic experiences, the more did readers and critics feel out of breath and blame him for sacrificing to metaphysics so much picturesque material. Be it added that Melville had hoped, when commencing to write, to earn a living for himself and for his family, and that from this motive was born his frenetic activity of a decade, a frenzy that was not without effect on his physical and mental health. But, as if every new book were a more relentless effort to exhaust the universe, embracing materials ever more vast and unexplored and, at the same time, continually complicating the mazes of his expression (by that law of analogy which would have the structure of the single sentence repeat that of the whole), there chanced to fall to the lot of the readers and reviewers the task of reminding him that society gives nothing for nothing, and that he who wants to be acclaimed by it must either amuse it or spoil it. It was, in short, a simple misunderstanding, and yet from the time of *Moby-Dick* (1851) Melville seems to have lost every illusion and, while on the one hand he begins to air his opinions about burying himself in an office, on the other hand he has already made up his mind to confront in his last books the most impossible themes in the most impossible of styles.

But whatever be the judgment pronounced upon the works of this feverish twilight, "Benito Cereno" belongs, by a now common consensus, to Melville's best vein. In the first place, it is a story of the sea, and the sea never betrays Melville's imagination. It is curious how an experience lasting little more than four years, and concluded when he was twenty-six, invaded his entire soul, filtering down to affect the most secret roots. The most heterogeneous experiences take in his mind the flavor, the spaciousness, of the ocean. There is no spring of his sensibility that does not vibrate imaginatively, and sometimes through the subtlest resonances, in that salt atmosphere. The introduction to *The Piazza Tales,* which describes the rural retreat of Arrowhead among the Berkshire Hills, where Melville was reduced to spending the last ironic and hectic years of his career as a writer, contains passages like these: "No light shows from the mountain. To and fro I walk the piazza deck. . . . In December . . . I pace the sleety deck, weathering Cape Horn. . . . In summer . . . the blown down of dandelions is wafted like the spray, and the purple of the mountains is just the purple of the billows, and a still August noon broods upon the deep meadows, as a calm upon the Line; but the vastness and the lonesomeness are so oceanic, and the silence and the sameness, too, that the first peep of a strange house, rising beyond the trees, is for all the world like spying, on the Barbary coast, an unknown sail." As in the enormous *Moby-Dick,* so in this brief and perfect "Benito Cereno" the sea is much more than a setting: it is the visible face, infinitely rich in analogies, of the mysterious reality of things. And this is true not only in the familiar sense that, in being made poetry, any setting loses its documentary transparence and becomes an imaginative creation, but in the less familiar sense that the sea is here the only sensible form that to the eyes of Melville can worthily incarnate the dark and ironic demonic center of the universe. You might go so far as to say that the seas, the interiors, the anxieties, the voices, all that comprises the background of the singular day spent by Captain Delano on the *San Dominick,* is *technically* analogous to the background of certain episodes in Dante's *Purgatorio*—the climbing, the drowsiness, the springtime twilights, and the visions—symbol, more than image, of an opposed conception of things: the possible angelic spiritualization.

This is necessarily broad and applies not only to the present narrative but to all the major work of Melville, throwing light on the fact that every time he tried—as in *Pierre*— to express this bitter conviction otherwise than by conjuring up the ocean, he ended much less self-assured and persuasive. Concerning "Benito Cereno" it is enough to observe how the ocean in its unmoving tranquillity is a mirror—an infinite mirror—of the growing suspicions of Captain Delano. There is something fearful in the very calm of the sea and in the restrained behavior of the host; and the information, so many times repeated, that the disasters of the *San Dominick* had reached their climax during calms—the days of unmoving anguish—in the middle of the Pacific, forebodes that precisely in the deepest peace of the present day and in the vague apprehensions that accompany it Melville is heaping up the burden of his horrors and of his demonic negations. So even the altogether seamanlike honesty and simplicity of the scandalized Captain Delano constitute another of those tragic calms that interpose themselves before the final explosion of ferocity in men and things. Because, as previously in *Moby-Dick,* not even here must we be misled by that stamp of masculine power which is produced by all the actions, and especially by the conclusion. The triumph of justice is in "Benito Cereno" only illusory: the demonic Babo finds his appropriate victory in his sentence, and to convince yourself of it you need only think again of the final phrases of the story: "the head, that hive of subtlety, fixed on a pole . . . across the Plaza looked . . . looked towards the monastery, on Mount Agonia."

These main points established, all the rest follows. And it would be easy to trace out how a continuous play of images, of references, and of allusions, from page to page, compounds the pathetic and monastic figure of Don Benito, the indolent hero of tedium and of the unfortunate nobility. To him is in turn connected that background of Old Spain which Melville's fertile style manages to create through images of such intensity as sometimes to seem a symbolic undercurrent. Passages like the simile of the *saya-y-manta* or the description of the Spanish flag used for a barber's towel leap to the eye as functional in the structure of the imaginative world to which they belong. Melville's discourse tends to follow attentively inner reality in all its most delicate ramifications and at the same time to elevate these fugitive movements of the soul to an imaginative sphere of myth—in the case of "Benito Cereno" to an intense atmosphere of calm which is not peace but foreboding of the abyss. Thus it happens that in this most perfect among Melville's tales, as in any other literary masterpiece, the richness of invention is first of all enjoyed in the single sentence. In other words, every single image of this imagination reflects in itself, like the eye of the idol, the panorama of the whole work.

PREFACE TO THREE LIVES

If to create a style means to be a classic, this now thirty-year-old book by a living writer is well worth including in a collection which from narrative art has hitherto collected only the classics. *Three Lives* is indubitably a masterwork of style, one of those exemplary works with which there is initiated the creative life of a person who will make of expression the perpetual question and sometimes the monomania of all existence. Indeed they have, even in their spiritual freshness, a kind of rigidity, that green woodiness of adolescence, which seems inseparable from every early testimony of a new process in the expression of reality. And yet they are not the works of adolescence. Insofar as we are given to know, the author wrote them when she was nearer thirty than twenty, and after various and contrasting experiences of life and culture.

The book was born among unusual circumstances of ambience which are recalled for us in *The Autobiography of Alice B. Toklas,* which is the autobiography of Gertrude Stein herself. Having impatiently cut short her university studies in psychology and medicine, she had come with a brother from her native Pennsylvania to Paris in 1903, and here she was living on her income, frequenting exhibitions of art, acquiring canvases by young and obscure painters named Matisse and Picasso, making herself intimate with these painters and their world. She spoke French with them and lived in the French way, and she tried to forget America and to uproot and transplant herself. Instead, in those very years, during long walks through that wonderful Paris, she brooded over her English as something precious and secret, and so she fondled it, auscultated it, shaped it in rhythmical patterns, making it quiver and start like a living thing, trying to gather from the verbal enchantment the rich memories and experiences of her childhood and youth spent in the tranquil cities of Pennsylvania, of California, and of Maryland, which in imagination were blended into one, the Bridgepoint of these tales.

It is not without significance that the major artists of the early twentieth century—one thinks of Joyce who, nomad through Europe, insistently returns to the youthful image of his Dublin, or of Proust totally intent within his walls of cork to recall *le temps perdu*—should come together on this ground of isolation, of material detachment from the reality which inspires them, as if the material distance, and the completion in time, of their experiences, should give wings, scope, and depth to the evocation. We have here the process opposite to that of the naturalistic art which was so pleased with the plaster cast of real life.

Composed during a period of realistic and sentimental stagnation in American fiction, these *Three Lives* are preeminently the discovery of a language, of an imaginative rhythm which tends to become itself the argument of the tale, the spiritual boundary of a magic and motionless daily reality. The celebrated future phrase carried on Stein's stationery, table napkins, and saucers—"a rose is a rose is a rose"—begins to peep out here in the cadence of certain pages, especially the most complex pages of the story of Melanctha. Along this road of the serene verbal obsession Gertrude Stein will go far and it will not always be easy to follow her. Already, here, in these tales, you sometimes feel the human material tremble and become a pure form which contemplates and transcends itself. Later there will come the pure inhuman style where life, here miraculously suspended, will evaporate, leaving a residue of dead cadences and psychological flashes. But whatever is the significance of her subsequent development—and especially of the most ambitious work, *The Making of Americans*—it seems to me that Gertrude Stein had given, with *Three Lives,* a perfect early example of what will be the constant goal of American fiction in the new century: an imaginary world which is reality itself, caught in the process of becoming expressive.

And it is important to observe that nothing is more alien to the manner of the book than the soliloquizing lyricism of so many twentieth-century writers. Even in its cadences and mazes, the page remains transparently sober and the vocabulary modest, as that of somebody who looks to the balance and truth of the sentence more than to a choice of diction. In this respect the form is entirely one with the meaning of the world evoked, which is the world of an almost biological normality and clarity.

This world, variously figured in the three tales according to the temperaments of the women who give them their titles, has its recurrent theme, almost a rhythm, in the calm and natural deaths of the protagonists. The author's idea is that every human being possesses a store of energy, a capacity of desires, of sensations, and of days. Having spent them, she dies, and nothing more can be done about it: death is an action perfectly clear and, precisely, biological. Without any of the hospital morbidities of so much of *our* literature, Stein reveals here something of her clinical education. She handles her women with the manner, infinitely compassionate but impersonal, of the good doctor, and the gentleness of her touch might often be mistaken for charity, but is not. Her charity is that of the nurse, of the loving compiler of charts. Like them, she knows how to detect and to value a fundamental normality of balance, and to it she deterministically reduces all life.

She ignores the drama of those who admit, like herself, the

finitude of each person but who are unwilling to resign themselves to it. She ignores the drama of the boundless will. Like all doctors, she is a master of prudence. In her pages life is terribly clear. For the sense of unmeasurable things, for the "imaginative," she substitutes the enchantment of the tranquil flowing, of being precisely a rose a rose a rose. The epigraph, "Donc je suis un malheureux et ce n'est ni ma faute ni celle de la vie," is the law of this tragic finitude; having used it up, you can die in peace.

ADDITIONS TO THE SECOND PREFACE TO MOBY-DICK

It is still necessary to recognize the complexity of this Melvillean culture, which at times ("Jonah Historically Regarded") seems to play with its own highest inspiration. In addition to being a moral myth, the fable of Moby Dick is also a sort of oceanic zoological and whaling treatise, and a poem of action and of peril. Indeed, some recent readers find in this tone its truest fascination.

The long cetological disquisitions, the descriptive minutiae on details of the chase and of navigation, the insistent and tongue-in-cheek digressions of every kind, not only testify to the many-stranded inspiration of the author, but they induce us to reflect on the singular interlacing of these motifs with the previously mentioned biblical motifs. It is undeniable that Melville's stylistic and structural effort was entirely directed to effectuate this adaptation, and the success of it seems to me equally undeniable. Every chapter, every sentence, every phrase of the book has that inevitable and fatal air which is like a classic seal. In the almost seventeenth-century luxuriance of his inventions and of his images, we will wish to cut or to tone down nothing. We pass from the supernatural terror which "The Spirit-Spout" or "Queequeg in his Coffin" inspire to the entertaining oddity of the researches on "The Fossil Whale" and of the gossips on "The Gam," and we don't feel any effort. The imaginative or rationalistic language of Melville always absorbs in itself without residue the entire life of the book, connecting itself to it by subtle filaments, by the allusiveness of a recollection, an echo, a rhythm.

Now this success is understandable only if you keep in mind the meaning of Ahab's myth. He pursues Moby Dick through a desire for vengeance, clearly, but, as happens in every infatuation of hatred, the longing for destruction appears almost a longing for possession, for knowledge, and, in its expression, in its outlet, is not always distinguishable from it. If we then recall that Moby Dick sums up in himself the mysterious quintessence of the horror and of the evil of the universe (see any one of Ahab's delirious monologues), we will doubtless have understood how all the digressive explanations, rationalistic and scientific, are not set against the Puritan fear of the divine unknown, but rather cloak it in a brilliant aura of effort, of inquiry, of cognitive fury, which is, as you might say, the secular reflection of it. The coherence of the book celebrates itself precisely in this tension which the fugitive shade of the mystical Moby Dick induces in his pursuers. At this point I want to praise the delicacy of which Melville gives evidence in leaving indefinite the meaning of his allegory. The commentators have been able to satisfy their own whims and to see symbolized in the monster an infinite variety of conceptions. That is a matter of no importance. The richness of a fable resides in the capacity which it possesses to symbolize the greatest number of experiences. Moby Dick represents a pure antagonism, and therefore Ahab and his Enemy form a paradoxical pair of inseparables. After so many disquisitions, so many treatises and so much passion, annihilation before the sacred mystery of Evil remains the only form of communion possible.

To render the meaning of this inevitable catastrophe, Melville leaves untried no strand of his culture, from the aforementioned terrifying biblical rhythms to the dry and eighteenth-century strength of the informational chapters, from the humorous fancy of the digressive pauses, which irresistibly remind us of so much nonfictional literary prose, to the high and Shakespearean imaginative tension of certain dramatic scenes. What coordinates and harmonizes all is the rich and skillful phrasing, vibrant with resonances, with echoes, with perspectives, just as the myth is a pregnant creation that reconciles successive spiritual spheres.

THE DEAD AT SPOON RIVER

Fernanda Pivano has translated *Spoon River Anthology* and has supplied for it a curious preface which implies more than it says. The translation, on the other hand, is explicit; all suffused with an innocent joy of discovery, it fascinates and persuades. If this is, as it seems, Pivano's first literary labor, I may say that seldom has a young writer been so well able to contain her enthusiasms and to chasten her pleasure with so much awareness. It looks like the labor of an expert authority, whom long and loving acquaintance with the text has taught to select and transfigure, in calmness of memory, the places of the soul. Some of these poems seem little by little to have become Italian, before the act of translation, in the insistent recurrences of the memory. So the discussion that accompanies the poems, rich with insights and fleeting references, seems to imply a previous, matured assimilation of a great part of the culture that produced them.

As it appears, not many Italians had news of this book. I remember only a short notice by Cecchi in *Ronda,* an admiring estimate in *America amara,* Vittorini's notice in the first *Americana,* and my old note in *La Cultura.* This book had the privilege of never coming to us involved in the petty and almost always unfair polemic which was our reaction to that culture. It never came up for discussion either in connection with the cinema or in connection with shocking realism. Perhaps it was protected by its ambiguous expressive simplicity, that singular mixture of journalistic juices and fermentings that, filtered and set in apparently artless forms, sometimes yields to the touch exactly a sound of old pottery. Our polemicists pass by, not finding there that timbre of facile and crude barbarism which they are accustomed to require from all twentieth-century transatlantic manifestations. In this connection, it is notable that in the preface the translator has resisted the temptation to give us a solemn catalog of sources, near and remote, for the book. So much the more notable because they leap to the eye. We have instead something better, a compendious reference to the themes and attitudes that the *Anthology* provoked or clarified for its contemporaries and successors. From 1915, the year in which it appeared, until 1940—in brief, the period between the two wars—there is no significant writer of that country who doesn't owe something of his message and of his world to Lee Masters. To speak of this book is thus to return to the source of some of the most vivid poetic experiences of our adolescence, to the heroic period when for the first time we cast a glance at a marvelous world which seemed to us something more than a culture: a promise of life, a call of destiny. Past history. Still, we are grateful to the young translator for having, with her frank and measured discourse, put us once again face to face with this lost image of ourselves.

In its complexity the *Anthology*—and the selection from it that Pivano gives us preserves this complexity, in fact I would say it increases its richness and its flavor—is an indispensable central link in that whole tangle of movements, influences, actions and reactions, which connects nineteenth-century American literature with that of the early twentieth century. In this respect, it is not inferior to the work of Emily Dickinson or to the *Three Lives* of Gertrude Stein. Probably it is more important, but its ambiguous power of characterization deprived it of a greater emphasis, as a result of which the boundaries in it between song and story are not always easily traceable, and more than one epitaph seems like a novelist's hurried note, rather than the tormented lyric investigation which it really is. Stein and Dickinson resolutely pressed forward along the road of experimental explorations, and, after the inevitable limbo of oblivion, they have reemerged as a brilliant mirage to the young generations obsessed with problems of art. Lee Masters' temperament was quite different; stirred by cultural and moral interests far more serious in their range, he didn't so much pursue the new poetic ways as, contenting himself once and for all with a given form—the epitaph—somewhat as poets of the past used to accept a meter, he concentrated his visionary faculties on the ethical tensions of his characters, the dead at Spoon River, asking them to reveal to him the secret, the final consciousness of their actions, and in this severe, Dantesque yearning he lived his imaginative anguish. How, at this point, can we fail to recognize in him the lineage of Hawthorne and Melville, indefatigable and misanthropic inquisitors of the heart's secrets and of the dilemmas of the moral life? In the same way that in Gertrude Stein or in Sherwood Anderson, in their rhythms and in their predilection for an exasperated and surrealistic normality, almost biological, we can hear again the echo—feminized and sophisticated, if you like, but I don't like—of the declamations and raptures of a certain Walt Whitman toward the "divine average." There remains in Lee Masters a shadow of the abstract fanaticism of the Puritan fathers, but not more than a shadow: the fierceness with which he constrains a poor wretch to look his destiny in the face is no longer theological, and seems rather to imply a stoic indignation, an appeal to a possibly truer human awareness. Faulkner and Hemingway are at the doors.

> And then I knew I was one of Life's fools,
> Whom only death would treat as the equal
> Of other men, making me feel like a man.

In her search for the laws of this poetry, the translator concludes that it consists in the discovery of the dimension of memory: "reality is seen under the aspect of memory" (p. xi). The remark seems to me obvious but inadequate, as does another, namely, that Lee Masters fixed "with clear and pitiless eyes *uomo americano,* localizing him in a province, with an intention more symbolic than descriptive" (p. ix). It seems to me that in this way the material of the book can be defined, and especially the material of that beautiful introductory poem, "The Hill," a *ballade du temps jadis* of new coinage:

Where are Ella, Kate, Mag, Lizzie and Edith,
The tender heart, the simple soul, the loud, the proud, the happy one? . . .

One died in shameful child-birth,
One of a thwarted love,
One at the hands of a brute . . .

but not the structure, the particular "outburst" of Lee Masters' imagination, as they appear in this whole gallery of human vices and virtues. In it there pass in review many diverse experiences and diverse temperaments—lovely women, ignorant brutes, ambitious political hacks, frustrated intellectuals, dissatisfied wives, libertines, young boys, old men, scientists—and how does Lee Masters' imagination manage to take fire from these facts and carry a coherent unity into the chaos?

Between a poem like

HAROLD ARNETT

I leaned against the mantel, sick, sick,
Thinking of my failure, looking into the abysm,
Weak from the noon-day heat.
A church bell sounded mournfully far away,
I heard the cry of a baby,
And the coughing of John Yarnell,
Bed-ridden, feverish, feverish, dying,
Then the violent voice of my wife:
"Watch out, the potatoes are burning!"
I smelled them . . . then there was irresistible disgust.

I pulled the trigger . . . blackness . . . light . . .
Unspeakable regret . . . fumbling for the world again.
Too late! Thus I came here,
With lungs for breathing . . . one cannot breathe here with
    lungs,
Though one must breathe. . . . Of what use is it
To rid one's self of the world,
When no soul may ever escape the eternal destiny of life?

and one like

FIDDLER JONES

The earth keeps some vibration going
There in your heart, and that is you.
And if the people find you can fiddle,
Why, fiddle you must, for all your life.
What do you see, a harvest of clover?
Or a meadow to walk through to the river?
The wind's in the corn; you rub your hands
For beeves hereafter ready for market;
Or else you hear the rustle of skirts
Like the girls when dancing at Little Grove.
To Cooney Potter a pillar of dust
Or whirling leaves meant ruinous drouth;
They looked to me like Red-Head Sammy
Stepping it off, to "Toor-a-Loor."
How could I till my forty acres
Not to speak of getting more,
With a medley of horns, bassoons and piccolos
Stirred in my brain by crows and robins
And the creak of a wind-mill—only these?
And I never started to plow in my life
That some one did not stop in the road
And take me away to a dance or picnic.
I ended up with forty acres;
I ended up with a broken fiddle—
And a broken laugh, and a thousand memories,
And not a single regret.

what is the common manner, the cut of the stylus? I should say that Lee Masters has seen in both cases the inexorable ensemble of actions, thoughts, and relationships which make a destiny, and has organized them according to a rhythm which is this destiny itself, the active movement of the character's soul.

The characters are not always seen *in articulo mortis;* of Fiddler Jones, and of many others, the supreme instant is not even recorded; the religious solemnity of each epitaph remains entrusted to the intensity with which the biographical information coincides with the absolute and secret meaning of the soul.

For example, of the life of Dillard Sissman, we don't know much:

> The buzzards wheel slowly
> In wide circles, in a sky
> Faintly hazed as from dust from the road.
> And a wind sweeps through the pasture where I lie
> Beating the grass into long waves.
> My kite is above the wind,
> Though now and then it wobbles,
> Like a man shaking his shoulders;
> And the tail streams out momentarily,
> Then sinks to rest.
> And the buzzards wheel and wheel,
> Sweeping the zenith with wide circles
> Above my kite. And the hills sleep.
> And a farm house, white as snow,
> Peeps from green trees—far away.
> And I watch my kite,
> For the thin moon will kindle herself ere long,
> Then she will swing like a pendulum dial
> To the tail of my kite.
> A spurt of flame like a water-dragon
> Dazzles my eyes—
> I am shaken as a banner!

Still this voice indubitably differentiates itself from the others through its poetic and human concretion. Each of these dead carries in himself a situation, a memory, a landscape, a word, which is a thing unspeakably his own. Indeed, living as we all do in the world of things, facts, actions, which is the world of time, our unconscious and incessant effort is a tending, outside of time, toward the ecstatic moment which will make us realize our freedom. It happens therefore that things, facts, actions—the passing of time—promise us these moments, clothe them, incarnate them, and they become symbols of our liberated awareness. Each of us possesses a wealth of these things, facts, actions, which constitute the symbols of his fate—they are worth nothing of themselves, in their natural state, but they invite us, they call to us, they are symbols. You might say that for Lee Masters death—the end of time—is the decisive moment which, from the forest of personal symbols, has violently detached one of them, and has welded it, nailed it forever, to the soul.

In the light of this criterion, I entirely concur in the selection of the *Anthology* offered us. With a sure taste, the translator has distinguished in the chorus the truest, the loveliest, voices. As an old fan of this poetry, I proceeded to flip through the pages of the complete original and rarely have I happened to find omitted an epitaph that I would have wanted to preserve. Nor has there been lost, in the reduction, that play of references and cross-references, of existential connections that makes of the entire Spoon River necropolis an almost narrative whole, a sacred drama, "a life tormented by repressed instincts, concealed vulgarities, camouflaged cowardices" that "at a certain moment is capable of being transfigured into a vision of evangelical wisdom. . . . Only the simple souls manage to triumph over life: this seems to be the final message of the book" (p. xii).

At this point, I ought to be permitted to say that I envy the translator the genuine pleasure which she felt in this labor. The stylistic felicity, often creative, bears witness to it, the stylistic felicity which pervades many of these pages. Only he who knows the laconic cunning of the text, all interwoven with hints of dialect, implications of local mores, lyric dissonances and outbursts, can measure the rendering—the alchemy—of the completed labor.

Here, for example, is the sting of a rattlesnake:

I reached my hand, but saw no brier,
But something pricked and stung and numbed it.

Or the wounded bird (a quail):

> He turned right over, feathers ruffled,
> With some of the down of him floating near.

The Apollonian metamorphosis:

> An hour
> When I seemed to be turned to a tree with trunk and branches
> Growing indurate, turning to stone, yet burgeoning
> In laurel leaves, in hosts of lambent laurel,
> Quivering, fluttering, shrinking, fighting the numbness
> Creeping into their veins from the dying trunk and branches!

The decayed apple tree:

> With its . . . blasted branches,
> And shoots of green whose delicate blossoms
> Were sprinkled over the skeleton tangle.

The good life:

> [I] rambled over the fields where sang the larks,
> And by Spoon River gathering many a shell,
> And many a flower and medicinal weed—
> Shouting to the wooded hills, singing to the green valleys.

The stallion Billy Lee:

> Black as a cat and trim as a deer,
> With an eye of fire, keen to start,
> And he could hit the fastest speed
> Of any racer around Spoon River.

The septuagenarian who never dies:

> Who sat in a wheel-chair half alive,
> With her throat so paralyzed, when she swallowed
> The soup ran out of her mouth like a duck.

The advice of the stoic gambler:

It's mean to sit and fumble the cards,
And curse your losses, leaden-eyed,
Whining to try and try.

The libertine's hymn:

I would I had thrust my hands of flesh
Into the disk-flowers bee-infested,
Into the mirror-like core of fire
Of the light of life, the sun of delight.

The death of the good giant:

And laughingly flung my giant arms
Over the smooth steel lips of the top of the tower—
But they slipped from the treacherous slime,
And down, down, down, I plunged
Through bellowing darkness!

The shade of Homer:

A blind man . . . with a brow
As big and white as a cloud.

A childhood memory:

For many times with the laughing girls and boys
Played I along the road and over the hills
When the sun was low and the air was cool,
Stopping to club the walnut tree
Standing leafless against a flaming west.

I have transcribed these passages selected at random, just by opening the pages, and I hope the reader may feel in them the absolute immediacy, the value of direct and genuine expression. The text, in these examples at least, has truly been all absorbed, without residues. But it is far from my intention to offer by means of these fragments an anthology of the *Anthology*. I care too much about the structural and human interest of each character and of all Spoon River. Rather, I repeat, for fear that we might have forgotten it, this volume of lyrics adds up to a narrative, a drama. And this is, for us men of letters, its most burning modernity.

AMERICAN RIPENESS

We had been accustomed to consider the United States a country which entered world culture with an eloquent, persuasive, and unmistakable voice only in the decade that followed the great war, and the names of Dewey and Mencken, Lee Masters and Sandburg, Anderson, O'Neill, Van Wyck Brooks, Waldo Frank, Gertrude Stein, Dreiser, Carlos Williams, Hemingway, and Faulkner had seemed to us the sudden explosion, inexplicable and unexpected, of a social or academic crust that, despite occasional protests and cracks—something was known of a Poe and a Whitman—persisted intact from the origins of the colonies. We interested ourselves even in the problem of Puritanism, of its innate relations with industrial capitalism (the "inspired millionaire") and, despite the fact that Puritanism had never annoyed us excessively, we shared the senation of those "young Americans" of being reborn Adams, lonely and resolute, no longer issuing from Eden but from a jungle, disencumbered of all the baggage of the past, fresh and ready to walk on free ground. Twentieth-century American culture—especially that literature—used to seem to us the only ideal place of encounter and work. It was exalting to feel ourselves uprooted and primordial while in the midst of the fraternal commotion of an extremely rich, complacent, and complex civilization. But now it turns out that those young Americans had made a mistake. Their explosion was not the first nor, more importantly, the greatest of American history. To them it had seemed otherwise, because when you revolt you need the illusion of doing an unprecedented thing; and we had believed them, because (among other things) we were seduced by their human warmth. But in reality it was not American culture that radically renewed itself in those years; it was we who touched it seriously, with the bare hand, for the first time. Now not a day passes without there eagerly coming to us from beyond the Atlantic voices which recall, evoke, and explain a whole, rich, century-long tradition, in which at least one great revolution, one great "renaissance," had already taken place. These war years were especially favorable to the inquiry, toning down a little the euphoria of individual invention and accustoming many American brains to rethink their own past, to question it about the present and about the future: in brief, to make history of it.

And now there reaches us a huge book, published in 1941 by the Oxford University Press, *American Renaissance* by F. O. Matthiessen, which offers a notable monument of this critical habit. The importance of this work goes beyond the peculiar problems of American culture, however novel and exciting they are to us, and makes of them a model of assumption and method even for us, who until yesterday were persuaded with difficulty to recognize critical mastery in anybody who wasn't the pupil of our own idealistic humanism. It is nice that this lesson should come to us precisely from America, from a culture, that is to say, which we have habituated ourselves to consider colonial, slipshod, and childish. At least in this instance, the fabled naiveté of the Americans shows itself in purity of perception and an instinctive preference for the living, the essential. The author was already well known for a subtle essay on T. S. Eliot, and in the new book he gives rich evidences of his sympathetic acquaintance with the most daring poetics of our time. In fact, in its very marrow, in the tortuous paths that cross it like a forest, it is nothing else than a study of the poetics of the five greatest nineteenth-century American writers. Such is Matthiessen's happy assumption, to take departure from a fact so obvious that no one had noticed it: the five most significant works of that nineteenth century appeared in the compass of a brief five years.[1] And Matthiessen, convinced that in the entire course of American culture there exists no other group of works which equals these in "imaginative vitality," asks himself "*what* these books were as works of art," and analyzing their material, their conscious and unconscious intentions, their effects, and their relations with the economic, social, cultural background, and with one another, ends by substantially clarifying what the unexpected flowering was and what it contributed to America and to civilization.

There is an evident agreement between the poetics of the five writers and Mattheissen's taste: the desire "that there should be no split between art and the other functions of the community, that there should be an organic union between labor and culture." And more clearly: " 'In a democracy there can be but one fundamental test of citizenship, namely: Are you using such gifts as you possess for or against the people?' " (pp. xv–xvi). Which explains the exclusion of the sixth great writer of the period, Poe—apart from the fact that he died in 1849. Poe inaugurated the tradition of art for art's sake and was "bitterly hostile" to democracy (p. xii), and therefore he could not enter the field of an inquiry so conditioned. Matthiessen does not ignore the vital contribution that Poe with his "narrow but intense theories of poetry and the short story" made to French symbolist culture, and from it, by repercussion, to the most recent American and British poetry, but he insists that this development ought really to constitute the argument of another book, extraneous to the problems which

1. 1850: *Representative Men* by Emerson, *The Scarlet Letter* by Hawthorne; 1851: *Moby-Dick* by Melville; 1854: *Walden* by Thoreau; 1855: *Leaves of Grass* by Whitman.

the Transcendentalism of Emerson, in the discussion of the social functionality of expression, the identification of the word with the thing represented, and the inevitability of symbolism, raised for himself and for his contemporaries.

For here is the substance of our book. That demand for an "organic union between labor and culture" which, variously expressed and relived, forms the common moral gound of the five writers, reveals itself from the opening bars as what really matters: the demand for a new language which, destroying the barriers between things and words, invests with intellectual light the most ordinary aspects of daily life and reveals their deep symbolic nature. The innumerable specific analyses, the play of the references and comparisons, the sounding of the most ingenious sources (the authentic readings of Hawthorne's diary, retouched and censored by embarrassed editors, or the underlinings and fevered marginalia that Melville scattered on the pages of his library)—everything tends to confirm and to clinch this obsession of the creative life of the five: to arrive at a language that would so identify itself with things as to batter down every barrier between the common reader and the most vertiginous symbolic and mythic reality.

Matthiessen well knows that at this point it is nonsense to invoke the primordial nature of *homo americanus,* his lack of traditions, his romantic privilege of having found himself at the beginning of history. Granted, for the sake of argument, that American culture was at that time unaware of a tradition, still it was weighed down with the cumbersome baggage of European academic culture which, felt as nonautochthonous, seems to have been made on purpose to provoke tortuous problems about what was truly American and to put in question, in a sophisticated way, principles and terms that to us Europeans appeared and appear unquestionable (pp. 474–475). But the fact is that America—Transcendentalist America of the Atlantic seaboard—was groaning under the weight of the tradition, a provincial tradition, of self-government, of public oratory and controversy, theological and political, which will even yet run the risk of turning at least two of our five writers (Emerson and Whitman) into complacent preachers. And here Matthiessen opportunely quotes (p. 206) Yeats's remark that "whenever language has been 'the instrument of controversy,' it has inevitably grown abstract." Tracts, sermons, political pamphlets, hortatory and instructive verses—this is the tradition and the culture, not in the least epic and primordial, out of which the literary explorations of the five writers rise in a passionate desire for concreteness and for life. Nor is it reckless to declare that the determining factor of this crisis was the newly acquired national consciousness of a democratic reality and mission. It is a little like what happened in ancient Rome, when only in the light of its unifying mission in the Mediterranean world were tongues loosened and the first poems sung, those poems that the long ages of happy poetical barbarism had never dreamed of creating.

The search for a new language naturally assumed various forms among the five writers, and in these pages the originality or monomania of each is clearly articulated and made to come alive. But it is natural that inquiry should first of all try to define the shared traits of the development. In an illuminating comment upon one of the most unforgettable pages in *Moby-Dick* ("The Mat-Maker"), the suggestive felicity of this style, and by implication the entire new sensibility under discussion, is defined as the technique of depicting, not thoughts but the mind thinking—in the words of Pascal—*la peinture de la pensée*. Matthiessen recalls the "metaphysical poets" of the English seventeenth century, who through Sir Thomas Browne so vivaciously colored Melville's style, and remarks that for them " 'an idea separated from the act of experiencing it is not the idea that was experienced' " (p. 130). This new attention to the creative process, this rich awareness of the level at which the imagination stirs, is the secret of all the poetic or narrative art of the new American age. Perhaps I may be permitted to recall that as early as 1933, in a study of Walt Whitman, I pointed out that in his poetry "every thought is really thought on the instant, the verse made of the daring and diversity of the mind in action, which beholds itself in the act of thinking the thought, and expresses its consciousness of it. Walt Whitman sings the joy of discovering thoughts." [2]

Nor does it escape Matthiessen that this obsession with the creative process, through which the process itself becomes material for poetry, had its roots in the futility, felt as such, of the national poetic tradition, in the absence of any vital "work," as a result of which futility and absence—and it happens even to Poe—the artist intensively reexamined the bases of his technique and literary theory and arrived at discoveries that anticipated contemporary European developments (p. 144). There is an important chapter of the book devoted to Horatio Greenough, the American sculptor who died in 1852 leaving wretched neoclassical statues and many scattered pages of discussions and reminiscences, from which, enthusiastically rediscovered in the twentieth century by Van Wyck Brooks, and from his conversations, as noted in Emerson's Journals, there emerges, self-aware and suggestive, the theory of the "organic principle." Greenough knows perfectly well that in America, " 'though the country was young, yet the people were old, that as Americans we have no childhood, no half-fabulous, legendary wealth, no misty, cloud-enveloped background. . . . [We forgot that] reason had been the dry nurse of the giant offspring, and had fed her from the beginning with the strong bread and meat of fact; that every wry face the bantling ever made had been daguerreotyped, and all her words and deeds printed and labelled away in the pigeon-holes of official bureaux' " (p. 146). Is it still necessary to quote here Emerson, Thoreau, or Whitman? But having established this position, unique in the history of the world, Greenough knows how to draw from it, more clearly than anyone else, the American consequence: the new art must be functional to this new

2. "Interpretation of Walt Whitman, Poet," *La Cultura,* July–September 1933 [p. 140 of the present volume].

reality according to the principle that " 'God's world has a distinct formula for every function, and . . . we shall seek in vain to borrow shapes; we must make the shapes, and can only effect this by mastering the principles' " (p. 146). Which means that in America only he will be a creator who is altogether drenched with the democratic principle. But the "functions" in a healthy democracy are not the feeble chatter of reformers and theorists, all of them people who had " 'no wholesome, working, organic relation with God's ground or with . . . [their] fellow men' " (p. 151). The magnificent and terrible energies of men must find their completion in organization. Not even the brute vitality of the savage ought to be shaken off from the civilized man but " 'must be assimilated and absorbed' " (p. 151). It is on these premises that Greenough finds, in agreement with Emerson, that the best expression of modern architecture is in his age a ship, the "yankee cutter" (p. 152). Like Melville and Whitman, Greenough understood that beauty can result only from energy, only from organic functionality.

One characteristic of this organic immediacy appears to be common among at least the most vigorous three of the five writers, Thoreau, Melville, and Whitman, and that is the preference for the verbs of action which crowd their most imaginative and introspective pages in the place of adjectives and abstractions (pp. 430 and 568). Through Melville, Matthiessen derives this preference from the stylistic example of Shakespeare, fellow demigod, and in a very fine analysis (pp. 421–431) he lays bare all the tangle of roots and veins which grafts the whaleman's major work to the pages of Shakespeare. But further on in the book, in a chapter devoted to the lively and burlesque sagas of the popular American tradition anticipating the tales of Mark Twain and O. Henry (pp. 635–645), we discover with amazement the very same style being adopted, in his coarse dialect, by George W. Harris (1814–1869), the rhapsodic creator of Sut Lovingood. In comedy he possesses the same tragic gifts of Melville: "the rare kind of dramatic imagination that can get movement directly into words" (p. 644). Irresistible passages are quoted.

Now on the level of a reflective and self-conscious art, this kinetic-functional energy is the happy result of a broader theoretical quest. Having conceived the universe as an Emersonian or Whitmanian mine of emblems or of absolute facts that the new Adam need only name, evoke, to make them come alive (pp. 41 and 44), it is clear that the more abundantly and variously you express the life of the senses, so much the more profound and comprehensive will be the panorama, the spiritual forest that riots within and presses for an exit to the light (p. 286). Things unsought and multiplied by perceptive subtlety will offer a seedbed of symbols always richer. Besides, the American tendency to find a spiritual meaning in every fact precedes and includes even the Transcendentalism of Emerson. It goes back to the religious origins of the nation, to the seventeenth-century habit of seeing the hand of Providence, the divine wrath, in the most banal and ordinary incidents, "in every capsized dory or runaway cow" (p. 243). Unless you also want to invoke the contemporary European culture which, from Swedenborg to Goethe to Carlyle, so much stimulated these writers. Anyhow, the fact is that romantic aesthetics had already "arrive[d] at mythology through the study of the origins of language" (p. 628). And Emerson knew that " 'language is fossil poetry.' " All of Matthiessen's five writers are scholars, heroic lovers of words, but they toil after the mot juste in a sense quite different from Flaubert's. Here is the whole difference between American "realism" and that of Europe. In the twentieth century, when at the time of the second renaissance from which we took our start in this essay, they return to talk of "realism" in self-conscious derivation from the naturalistic French school, the thing will be clearer: the realism of Lee Masters, of Anderson, of Hemingway, will variously seek the whole man, that second reality which underlies appearance; it will seek to "name" things in order to release from them the explosive spiritual charge, and for this realism it will not be appropriate to speak of province or *tranche de vie*. Nor does Matthiessen ever forget to make intelligent and provocative references to these later writers (pp. 85, 393, 592, and passim).

Thus the desire and the need for a language at the same time rich and precise—yet even here a difference. These writers have no pedantry, not even the pedantry of the vernacular. Their diction is composite, drawn from technical terms and the common language but also from the pages of the most elegant poets of the seventeenth century and from the Bible. Not even Whitman, who so often called for the use of simple, ordinary "average and vulgar American," knew then how to limit himself to this language; he only occasionally derived from it certain lively and pithy idioms. In reality, he was searching precisely in the "slang" of laborers, rail-road men, miners, drivers, farmers, boatmen, for the capacity to " 'approach a meaning' . . . by the circuitous routes of lively fancy" (p. 526). It is he, besides, who, taking up again Thoreaus's pregnant word "indirection," the method of looking at things " 'with the unworn sides of the eye' " (p. 90), argues that the poet must seek to avoid "bald literalism, and express . . . [himself] illimitably" (p. 519). What does this mean? "Indirection" is that method by which the writer will be neither descriptive nor epic but transcendent—in other words, symbolic (p. 519). For the new symbolism of Whitman and his generation consisted precisely in this: not the ambitious allegorical structures of plot and of formulation—those of a Bunyan or of a Dante—but a different verbal reality, a sort of double vision through which from the single object of the senses, avidly absorbed and possessed, there radiates a sort of halo of unlooked-for spirituality. Even in his most dangerous cases, such as the successive levels of the structure of a *Moby-Dick,* Matthiessen knows how to direct the light of this principle: and with satisfied amazement we read in a letter from Melville to Hawthorne's wife that the author managed to see all the allegorical fine points of his great book only when he had already written it and was reading the comment of his friend upon it (p. 250).

But how the abundance of ordinary American life is the ideal goal of this new literature is made clear especially in the part devoted to the analysis of Whitman's rhythms and analogies (Book IV). Since Emerson never decisively confronted the real and Hawthorne preferred to shut himself up in his enchanted manse, there remain, to furnish the highest proofs of the new aesthetic, the other three, and of them the least trammeled in humanistic tradition, which might complicate the inquiry, is undoubtedly Whitman. The enormous sensory and geographical panorama of his "songs" seems an ever-renewed attempt to see reality as a play of primordial organic forces which live insofar as the poet identifies himself, incarnates himself mythically in them. And this incarnation, this embrace, has an insistent, though chaste, sexual tone. Matthiessen can quote:

(p. 570) I moisten the roots of all that has grown.
(p. 570) Stand at my side till I lean as high as
I can upon you,
Fill me with albescent honey, bend down to
me,
Rub to me with your chafing beard, rub to
my breast and shoulders.
(p. 570) The curious roamer the hand roaming all
over the body, the bashful withdrawing
of flesh where the fingers soothingly
pause and edge themselves.
(p. 618) Bridegroom night of love working surely and
softly into the prostrate dawn,
Undulating into the willing and yielding
day,
Lost in the cleave of the clasping and
sweet-flesh'd day.
(p. 566) The souse upon me of my lover the sea, as
I lie willing and naked.

In order to give voice to America, the bloodless language of Puritan controversy had to arrive at this point. Matthiessen estimates how much of the preponderantly oratorical education of the time enters into this poetic (and discovers the already-existing identification of the speaking voice and personality): " 'who touches this book touches a man' " (pp. 554–555); how broadly a taste for opera was already diffused among the American populace (pp. 558–563); how much of that subtler experience of rhythm which the sea, the cadences of natural phenomena, the pulsing of the blood, sex, the alternation of the days and the nights, the comings and goings of the crowds, insinuated into the poet's consciousness (pp. 564–577). From the pages of Thoreau—more exclusive, more limited, but also more impeccable—analysis had already brought forth, earlier in the book, the younger and more austere sister of the Whitmanian ode (pp. 113–118).

But also in the other greatest writer, Melville, there is seen the deep inspiration in these same obscure life-giving forces which the abstract American lust for the ideal has atrophied under the most diverse forms. In him and in Hawthorne, the narrative artists, viewed as "tragic" vis-à-vis the Transcendental optimism of the other three, the preachers (and this is one of the few instances of residual formalism in the book), there are also examined in depth even their systems of moral relations, their anthropologies, and their social-political convictions. But it is implicit in investigations so conducted that in the majority of cases the results remain pure document. A general correspondence between the diffused ideology of a society and the structure and orientation of its creative energies and myths is one thing, and it is quite another thing to connect the character of a style or a gesture with the opinions of a writer on the war in Texas or on the representative system. Here you walk on shifting sands. Still, even on this subject of the profound tragic seriousness of the two narrative artists, our book knows how to conclude with a persuasive word (p. 349): "This perception of the double nature of life, of the fact that there is no such thing as good unless there is also evil, or of evil unless there is good" is not enough to make a tragic writer. The tragic writer's power "springs not from the mind's recognitions, but from the depth to which the writer's emotions have been stirred by what he has recognized, from the degree to which he has really been able to comprehend and accept what Edgar meant by saying,

> Men must endure
> Their going hence even as their coming hither:
> Ripeness is all."

It is the sentence which Melville underlines in his copy of *King Lear*. And it seems to me a worthy epigraph and conclusion of the long discourse on the first truly "mature" Pleiad of young America.

A USEFUL BOOK

He who is not of the craft, or at least of the milieu, always thinks that just that method of storytelling, of narrating, of painting, which is most frequently met and which requires the least effort to understand and to take an interest in, is the only true and legitimate method, and that it has always been this way. Men, it is said, have always had two arms and two legs, the flavor of bread and wine has always been what we know them to be, babies have been born in identical fashion, and from time out of mind the sun warms and the water wets. There is then one way to write novels, to paint pictures, to make music, which is like that bread and that wine, that sun and that water, and this way is that customary way which satisfies the greatest number, which appears natural and immediate, like the bread and the wine, like the gestures that everyone makes, like the rotation of the seasons. The rest, the experiments, innovations, originalities, the "modern arts," are a waste of time and a nuisance, a presumption, futurism.

But, putting the question so, all see where it is going to end. The paintings, the music, the most indisputable books of the past, *Iliads, Divine Comedies,* Greek tragedies, ought to reach us and please us with the same facility with which we accept the latest film, the latest play, the latest Hungarian novel. And this—I swear—is not the case. Therefore, something in art has changed, and if it changed once, it changes still, and it always changes.

Babies, the seasons, the bread and the wine, don't enter into it. Here we are not in the world of nature, we are in history. "Art" is "technique," and everyone knows that a product of technique is something artificial, approximate, which incessantly tends toward perfection, to base itself on more exact and precise discoveries. "Art" is in sum "artifice," and in it nothing is given once and for all; every age takes up again the question from the roots and creates again its own "modern art." Nothing in the field is ever definitive—not even *Aida* or the novels of Steinbeck.

This necessary lecture, addressed to those who are not of the craft, has for its intention to persuade the common reader of American novels (Lewis, Steinbeck, Hemingway, Faulkner, Caldwell, Saroyan, etc.) to read the autobiography of an American who was not a great novelist but who—since he was a very great writer—discovered an America and a way of being, of imagining, of writing, to which all the great narrative artists contemporary with him and after him owe something. *A Story Teller's Story* by Sherwood Anderson is a voyage toward the discovery of himself and the world, and that the hero is a writer, that is to say, who has preoccupations and thoughts different from the ordinary, ought not to alarm the well-disposed reader. Sherwood Anderon puts so much care and so much hearty desperation into his working day and is so mischievously sincere in describing the restlessness by means of which, after having passed through the usual many occupations (soldier, worker, stableboy, businessman), he discovers himself as a writer, that his becomes an intimate and imaginative story of an entire society. And this society is nothing less than America from 1890 to the First World War. The battle that Sherwood Anderson fights within himself to break and dissolve the bourgeois, American, industrial clichés, habits of mind, lazinesses, and idiocies, which used to weigh heavily (and which weigh still) on art, on fiction, on the inner life of that people, is retraveled by every reader as a new personal experience of liberation and historical understanding.

Having read this book, you will have learned something of the profound dignity and of the human value of every honest experiment by the writer who wants to renew himself, who wants to be himself; you will have caught the habit of not considering a work of literature only as an entertainment or a banality. But you will also have understood that the words, the sentences, the literary modes, are never adventitious, that they are never, like bread and wine, simple data of an unchangeable common sense: in them is reflected a whole economic, ideological, and social situation. Anyone who has class consciousness realizes this. But he must also realize that it is inconsistent to strive to renew the structure and ideologies of a given society, if he then continues to be happy with a style of painting, a way of making music, or of writing, clearly determined by an environment in my opinion already condemned.

A NEGRO SPEAKS TO US

The times in which we discovered America are finished. In the course of a decade, from 1930 to 1940, Italy not only made the acquaintance of at least half a dozen contemporary American writers whose names will remain, but also dug up again some of the nineteenth-century classics of that literature and glimpsed the radical continuity that runs under all the past and present manifestations of that people. It was also the decade in which it seemed that music and cinema were giving a fresh jolt to our spoiled European sensibility. The discovery was full of that thrill of liberation and scandal which is inseparable from any encounter with a new reality, and which the Italian and European political climate did its best to arouse.

Now it is finished. Now America, the great American culture, has been discovered and recognized, and it can be foreseen that for several decades nothing more will come from that people comparable to the names and revelations that enthused our prewar youth. The Americans know it, too, although they don't too often say so, and they devote themselves to a conscientious labor of cataloging and studying the twenty-year period between the wars. The truly important books that now come to us from beyond the ocean are no longer fiction or poetry but books of history, of interpretation, of comment. All the new writers have lost that wonderful expressive immediacy, that native sense of the land and of the real, that rough wisdom that once endeared to us a Lee Masters, a Hemingway, a Caldwell, and now they worry themselves in complicated simplemindednesses well known to us, which will perhaps yield some fruits in time, but for now they add nothing to our cunning as artful Europeans. As for the movies and the rest, it is better not to speak. In brief, it seems to me that today, after the war and the occupation, after having long sojourned and conversed among us, the young Americans have undergone an interior process of Europeanization, and have lost a great part of that exotic and tragic candor that was their destiny. But in the play of history, perhaps even this forms part of their destiny.

The fact remains, however, that when in these years there still arrives a good book from America, of the kind that touches you to the depths and constrains you to reexamine in a hurry and a frenzy experiences and convictions and past lazinesses—it is always a question of a delayed reaction—you look at the date and notice that the book, the novel, the tale, goes back to the period before the war, the generation that was shaped in those years. And so I want to speak of *Black Boy* by Richard Wright, which was published in 1937 in America, and which Einaudi is now publishing in Italy in a good translation.

Here we have an autobiography which extends from the author's first years to the end of his adolescence, precisely the twenty years of great American prosperity. But you search in vain in this book for any trace of big industry, of dynamic business, of fervor, and of turmoil. It is the story of a southern Negro, whose family lives in continuous straits and restlessly moves from hamlet to hamlet, from one relative to another, while the boy struggles amidst hunger, fears, school, and really useless jobs. But he who, loyal to the image of the Negro world provided by the theater, the movies, and the Anglo-Saxon orchestras, expects from the book dreamlike atmospheres, plantations, sensuality, black laughter, alleluias, will be deluded in the end. For the Negro writer there is nothing exotic in his environment. We move among Negro villagers, among wretchedly poor small-town people. This is the reader's first surprise: what takes place between the relatives and the boy, between the boy and his playmates, between the world outside those iron walls and incomprehensible taboos and the desire which the boy feels to live and to understand, in all this there is nothing fabulous or exotic but an experience which we have all had, an anxiety and a pain which we have suffered identically in our own families. From the absurd childish tricks which draw on the head of the young Richard affectionate and ferocious punishment to the gloomy boredom of the church services which the bigoted grandmother forces him to attend, it is all a story we know well. Perhaps some of us know less about the daily hunger cheated by gulping down some water or about the blind terror lest the white people, the "enemies," break loose and organize a lynching. Perhaps. When the book was written there were few Europeans, few white people, who knew about such things. But now? Is there anyone among us, any white person, who has not looked hunger and racial terror in the face, and who can swear that tomorrow these specters will not rise again?

This is the message, the truest word, of *Black Boy*, the authentic and suffered fruit of a human endurance and adventure which concerns everybody, and in a clear and dramatic language it seeks under our encrustations of rhetoric and of pride the manly capacity to look things in the face and to rethink the old admonition that every man in our neighbor. It happens, reading this book, that we keep forgetting that we are among Negroes, among black skins. The writer always goes to the heart of the matter and if, at a certain point, one of his Negro adolescents says in irritation that after all "white folks smell," that is a consequence, almost a caricature, of the white legend that it is the Negroes who smell. Every fault or brutality in the race (and there are many in the book) corresponds to an abuse of power or to an analogous prejudice of the white masters.

Certainly, the verbal means with which Richard Wright has told us this story of his entrance into life have served him wonderfully. We are in the tradition of the great prose narrative, that prose which never lingers over the pleasures or the coquetries of the craft, but strives to give to the page the rhythm and the conviction of the living voice, to express, along with the event, the excitement of the one who tries to understand and so to appease it. Clearly, our writer has not done it on purpose, but I often seemed to hear again, reading those pages, the miraculously energetic voice of a Defoe or a Cellini. And this also has led me to speak of him.

YESTERDAY AND TODAY

Around 1930, when Fascism was beginning to be "the hope of the world," some young Italians happened to discover in their books America—an America thoughtful and barbaric, happy and truculent, dissolute, fecund, heavy with all the past of the world, and at the same time young, innocent. For several years these young people read, translated, and wrote, with a joy of discovery and of revolt that infuriated the official culture; but the success was so great that it constrained the regime to tolerate it, in order to save face. Was it a joke? *We* were the country of resurrected Romanism, where even geometers studied Latin, the country of warriors and saints, the country of Genius by the grace of God; and how did these low-class types, these provincial businessmen, these upstart multimillionaires, dare give us a lesson in taste, getting themselves read, discussed, and admired? The regime endured it with clenched teeth, and meanwhile stood at the breach, always ready to profit from a false step, a page more crude, a blasphemy more direct, to catch us in the act and deliver the blow. It delivered a few blows, but indecisively. The flavor of scandal and easy heresy that surrounded the new books and their subjects, the intensity of revolt and of sincerity that even the most thoughtless felt pulsing in those translated pages, were irresistible to a public not yet entirely stupefied by conformism and the academy. You can certainly say that at least in the fields of fashion and taste the new fad helped a good deal to perpetuate and nourish the political opposition, however vague and futile, of the Italian "reading" public. For many people, the encounter with Caldwell, Steinbeck, Saroyan, and even with their forerunner Lewis, made the first little hole in the wall to freedom, the first suspicion that not everything in the world's culture ended with the fasces.

It hardly needs saying that, for those who knew, the real lesson was more profound. Those who didn't limit themselves to flipping the pages of a dozen or so startling books that issued from beyond the ocean during those years, but shook the tree to make it drop its hidden fruit also and then searched all around to discover its roots, were soon persuaded that the expressive wealth of that people was born not so much from an obvious search for scandalous and ultimately superficial social assumptions, but from a severe and already century-old desire to compress ordinary experience in language, without there being anything left over. From this motive sprang their continuing effort to readjust language to the new reality of the world, in order to create, in effect, a *new* language, down-to earth and symbolic, that would justify itself solely in terms of itself and not in terms of any traditional complacency. And of this style which, often vulgarized, still in the latest books surprised us by its unusual clarity, it was not difficult to discover initiators and pioneers in the poet Walt Whitman and in the narrator Mark Twain, who belong to the ninteenth century.

At this point American culture became for us something very serious and valuable; it became a sort of great laboratory where with another freedom and with other methods men were pursuing the same job of creating a modern taste, a modern style, a modern world that, perhaps with less immediacy but with just as much pertinacity of intention, the best of us were also pursuing. That culture seemed to us, in brief, an ideal place of work and exploration, of sweaty and anguished exploration, and not merely the Babel of noisy efficiency, of crude neon optimism, which deafened and blinded the naive and which, seasoned with some Roman hypocrisy, would not have been displeasing even to our provincial party bosses. During those years of study, it dawned on us that America was not "another" country, a "new" beginning in history, but only the gigantic theater where with greater freedom than elsewhere the drama of all was being acted out. And if for a moment it seemed worthwhile to repudiate ourselves and our past in order to give ourselves body and soul to that free world, that was because of the absurd and tragicomic condition of civil death into which history had for the moment driven us.

In those years American culture gave us the chance to watch our own drama develop, as on a giant screen. It showed us a furious fight, conscious, unceasing, to give a meaning, a name, an order, to the new realities and to the new instincts of personal and social life, to adjust to a world dizzyingly changed the ancient meanings and the ancient words of man. As was natural in times of political stagnation, we all limited ourselves to studying how those transatlantic intellectuals had "expressed" this drama, how they had come to "speak" this language, to "tell," to "sing," this fable. We could not openly participate in the drama, in the fable, in the problem, and so we studied American culture somewhat as one studies past ages, the Elizabethan dramas, or the poetry of the *dolce stil nuovo*.

Now times have changed and anything can be said, indeed it more or less *has* been said. And it happens that the years go by and there come from America more books than once, but today we open and close them without any excitement. Once even a minor book which came from there, even a B movie, moved us and presented us with living problems, wrung from us an assent. Is it we who have grown old, or has this little bit of freedom been enough to detach us? The poetic and fictional achievements of the American twentieth century will remain

—a Lee Masters, an Anderson, a Hemingway, a Faulkner now live in the heaven of the classics—but as for me, not even the fast of the war years was enough to make me fall in love with that which once more comes to us from over there. Sometimes it happens that I read a lively book which strikes the imagination and appeals to my conscience, and then I look at the date: prewar. In brief, I honestly think that American culture has lost its mastery, its innocent and knowing intensity that put it in the vanguard of our intellectual world. Nor can I but remark that the loss coincides with the end, or suspension, of its fight against Fascism.

After the most brutal prohibitions fell, we learned that many countries in Europe, and in the rest of the world, are today the laboratory where forms and styles are being created, and that nothing prevents those of goodwill, though they live in an old convent, from speaking a new word. But without a Fascism to which to oppose itself, that is to say, without a historically progressive idea to embody, even America, for all the skyscrapers and automobiles and soldiers it turns out, will no longer be in the vanguard of any culture. Without an idea and without the progressive struggle, it even risks giving itself to a kind of Fascism, although it be in the name of its best traditions.

THE GREAT AMERICAN ANGUISH

Edgar Lee Masters, who died recently in his eighties, after a full and richly productive life, is now himself a voice of Spoon River. To whom shall we compare him? To Petit, the poet, who used to warble "villanelles, rondels, rondeaus," while Homer and Whitman roared in the pines? To John W. Burlson, who married the banker's daughter and wrote essays, and frequented intellectuals, but could never write a line, a single enduring line? To Jack, the strolling fiddler who, in the great beyond, with all the other musicians, "from highest to lowest," seated at the foot of a blind man "with a brow as big and white as a cloud," listens to him sing of the fall of Troy? It is notable that like all, or nearly all, the other people of Spoon River, the poets are frustrated people, disappointed or resigned or timid. Lee Masters' own life seems not to have been that way, considering its external success and fruition. And it does not even seem that he was unaware of the thrill, the joy, of the great inspiration and vision—so many are the characters in his cemetery for whom a great memory, an ecstatic moment, vibrates in their bones. Why, then, in giving voice to the destinies of the three declared poets, has he touched accents so bitter and so pathetic?

'Tis vain, O youth, to fly the call of Apollo.
Fling yourselves in the fire, die with a song of spring,
If die you must in the spring . . .

says Webster Ford, the last voice in the book, Lee Masters himself, who is thinking over his life.

O leaves of me
Too sere for coronal wreaths, and fit alone
For urns of memory . . .

The sternest and most conscious poetry of Lee Masters inheres in this humiliated celebration of the energy and the youth of a great past. Not a lament for his own youth, for his own personal pride and pleasure, but a heroic dream of "the republic," of "giant hands [who] from the womb of the world tore the republic," the real "pioneers" who loved and fought with courage. To this dream Lee Masters gave a name, "Jeffersonian democracy," and in the course of his slow set of sun he wrote many historical and poetical books about its most memorable figures. In the second decade of the century, he thus originated a longing for, and a recollection of, the purest American tradition which so many writers were to take up again, a sure sign that the tradition was sinking to sunset, was already past history.

Is Lee Masters then a kind of Carducci, and Whitman, prophet of democratic energy and pioneer, his Dante? Up to a certain point. Carducci never managed to cross the boundaries of the third Italy and speak to the world; his dream of humanity was fed by scholastic and anticlerical provincial polemics. Lee Masters mercilessly regarded the "little America" of his time and judged it and represented it in a swarming human comedy where the vices and worth of each person spring from the parched and corrupted ground of a society whose involution is only the most clamorous and tragic example of an involution endemic to all Western civilization. Therefore, the sepulchral, sorrowful, terrible, sarcastic voices of Spoon River have moved us and touched us to the depths. It is the voice of a society that no longer thinks "in universals." Lee Masters told a reporter: "Every two or three years until recently he read all of the great Greek plays. 'The great marvel of the world is Greek civilization. They thought in universals, as did the Elizabethans.' "

To think in universals means to take part in a society, not where (as the fools think) sorrow, spiritual or physical anguish, the problematical nature of life, are abolished, but where there exist instruments to conduct a common, concerted fight against sorrow, misery, death. And Lee Masters testifies with his *Anthology* that the society in which he found himself living lacks these instruments, these "universals"—in other words, that it has lost the direction and control of its actions. Hence the futile and horrible tragedies that filled the cemetery on the hill.

There is a little episode in the life of the lawyer Lee Masters which can help us reflect upon the meaning of his work. In April 1914, when he began to compose the *Anthology,* he was defending in court a union of starving Chicago waitresses. Through that whole time he lived, as it were, a double existence. "Oh, I had vigor; I never was better in court. . . . But sometimes I'd look about the court, and everything was there in plain sight, yet I'd feel that I wasn't part of it. . . . I wrote the poems on menu cards, on the backs of letters, at home, in my law office. . . . Later I was offered $5,000 for the manuscript of 'Spoon River,' but a man doesn't keep menu cards. The manuscript was thrown away." It is nothing more than an episode, perhaps embroidered by the journalist who recounts it (Robert Van Gelder, *Writers and Writing,* 1946), but it seems to me symbolic of this man and of his work. The inexorable clarity of the American anguish is born in a hall of justice, while people argue the fate of humble waitresses on strike. So many are the roads of poetry.

APPENDIX: ENGLISH WRITERS

PREFACE TO DEFOE, *MOLL FLANDERS*

The Fortunes and Misfortunes of the Famous Moll Flanders was written by Daniel Defoe in his sixties, in the third of those extraordinary six years (1719–1724) in which he gave to the world, besides various pamphlets and tracts and biographies, *The Life and Strange Surprizing Adventures of Robinson Crusoe, The Adventures of Captain Singleton, A Journal of the Plague Year, The History and Remarkable Life of Colonel Jacque,* and *Roxana.* Such a luxuriance of creative energy came after an entire existence resolutely spent in the struggles of commercial enterprises, all different and all unsuccessful, and later, when he turned to politics and literature, tested by persecutions, imprisonments, exhausting labors at the writing desk, and above all poverty.

Nothing can render the temper of this man better than the frank and vigorous voices of his protagonists. They are all alike and the adventure of all is the same: whether children of rich merchants or poor orphans of the prison, they all face a life in which the harshness of their daily plight is equaled only by their tireless resolution; and the repeated and almost biblical desolations in which they are found naked and alone before the world and God take on the shape of tragic pauses from which their energy will emerge intact and even increased. These individuals are essentially alone. In this sense the wearisome solitude of Robinson Crusoe on the island is the most conspicuous and memorable myth of the solitude of each one.

The daily struggle of these people is not concerned with spiritual problems or with protoromantic ideals of passion. Defore has reduced to its most elementary form the tragedy of existence: "Give us this day our daily bread" is clearly the most insistent prayer that arises from every page of these autobiographies. It is less true that they also pray: "Lead us not into temptation"; or, at least, the genuine piety that gushes from these hearts after the most tremendous trials is only a quite human reflection of their need for security and material sufficiency.

These general considerations will seem no great novelty to Italian readers of *Robinson Crusoe* and *Captain Singleton.* But it seemed to me that I ought to recall them in presenting this first Italian translation of the life of Moll Flanders, because they will serve to put in relief the singularity of tone which I think Defoe has been able this time to impose upon his usual adventure of struggle, of sin, and of repentance. I mean this: the figure of Moll Flanders who, through the richness of her experiences, seems to me the most complex of all the characters the author has imagined, reveals in the precise and merciless calmness of her memories a capacity for irony which at times goes well beyond the obligatory compunction of the penitent. This capacity—be it said in passing—seems to me to detach Moll Flanders from the whole varicolored family of heroes of the eighteenth-century novel who always run to the extremes either of the generic or the characteristic. Above all, Moll judges herself in contact with a world which the national taste for sentimentaility and humor has not yet managed to deform and impoverish. Here the autobiographical form, chosen by Defoe perhaps for mere contingent reasons of literary custom, reveals a more profound poetic reason. Moll Flanders, and through her the author, feels toward none of the events or persons she falls in with—and so much the less toward herself—that witty and idle interest which schematizes reality in adventures and caricatures, even if these be called Tom Jones. Moll Flanders doesn't pause to jot down, amused and disturbed, characteristic words or gestures, but from each individual she gathers the essential significance incarnated in the real sorrow or the real joy which she has received from them. Especially, she treats herself in this way.

Now this attentive investigation of one's own motives and those of others, expressed with the implacable awareness of one who is accustomed to conclude the most desperate examinations of conscience with the detailed accounting in pounds sterling of her remaining means, is precisely what I call the irony of *Moll Flanders.* It is in the intermingling and in the fusion of these extreme motives that I think this irony consists. There is much to learn, Moll warns, from my trespasses and from my repentance: how the most solemn resolutions of virtue are in vain without the divine support, and "by what methods innocent people are drawn in, and plundered robbed, and by consequence how to avoid them." Let's perform our penance, the humble sinner seems to say, but let's keep our eyes open, because in the end God helps those who help themselves. In this respect, the most delightful pages are those of the final years in Virginia, where the favor of Heaven tangibly blesses, to the clink of sterling, the sage discretion of the wife of the two husbands. So that it is not then entirely clear if "Mistress Moll" owes her prosperous and serene old age more to the benevolence of Heaven than to the capacity, of which her existence is a very clear example, of concealing skeletons in the closet.

But I don't want to insist too much on this point lest I create the impression that the attractive Moll is an abstract and inhuman type of "Machiavellian" calculator, an impression which would, among other things, deprive her most unusual voice of all interest and resonance. She, and with her the author, takes life too seriously to be reduced to so superficial a scheme. Let the attentive reader notice—if I have succeeded in preserving in this translation the humble and severe vigor of this most modern of eighteenth-century English prose styles—all the rich gamut of tones in which these memories live again, from the ribald pages of advice for women in a hurry to get married to those penetrating and dreadful pages on the stay in Newgate and on her own death sentence. Even if there were nothing else, the open and sincere capacity for abandon of which she gives evidence in her adventure with the Lancashire husband would be enough to acquit Moll. To hear her, her whole existence has been one single aspiration for honesty, nor would she ever have been induced to evil if not constrained by the cruelest of needs. In this connection, the periods of time, which she usually dispatches with a few sentences, of her successive married lives, are revelatory, when, a minimum of security and comfort being given her, she becomes the most compunctious of Christians and the most reasonable of wives. It is however true that these periods pass through her memory like lightning, and that there succeed, detailed and implacable, her sorties and robberies against mankind. Well, and so what? She writes so that he who reads can find some instruction, if he would be pleased to treasure it up, and her whole experience keeps telling her that the most generous resolutions and the exercise of the most incontestable virtues irremediably disappear with the last pound sterling. All her life is thus spent in the presence of "the rainy day." And since no one will want to deny that she has plenty of rainy days, we will do well to grant her that initial sympathy of which we all have need.

PREFACE TO DICKENS, *DAVID COPPERFIELD*

In translating this book I have often chanced to think that our century will no longer write "human comedies," not really because it lacks that constructive vision of the world which so many call for but because we lack instead the necessary naiveté. For it takes an enormous, fundamental naiveté to place yourself in front of a human world, and to watch it live, listen to it talk, registering the occurrences with the same good-natured or misanthropic humor that accompanies us in a crowd. It was naive to think that the tumult of a crowd of people, rendered with as much care "as it is in life," could ever coincide with our imagination. The imagination, which is pure construction, used to display itself in characters, in caricatures, voices, and gestures, so much the more lifelike as they were the more invented, which the social reality, external and quotidian, of the narrative would take up in its course and allow to appear, deluding their creator into believing that they lived as in real life.

The great narrators of the first half of the century, especially Dickens and Balzac—before naturalism, just with its crudity, threw a visionary gleam on the most realistic pages—are all full of this naiveté, and therefore reading them is so pleasant and restful. With these writers, we enter tangible worlds historically documented where, each character with his singularity functioning as an imaginative nucleus, a whole tangle of candidly true events seizes them and composes them in photographic picturesque attitudes. All these characters have a strangeness—tenebrous mystery or simple tic—but none of the events they undergo has a significance or a construction. The fact is that the imagination—inexhaustible and unpredictable as long as these writers deal with human faces—as soon as these figures begin to move in "society" is extinguished in front of the mechanism of the real; and with naive faith in the events, the imagination watches them live a day that has no end, as it had no beginning. Indeed, these novels, perhaps just because they are always equipped with an Epilogue or a Conclusion, never have a true ending; and the synthetic summary that closes them contains material for pages and pages more.

David Copperfield is doubtless Dickens' novel in which the characterization is most capricious and the futility of the plot most enjoyable. A quite vast world is here evoked for us: bourgeois, sailors, housewives, swindlers, simple girls, lawyers, shopkeepers, maidservants, misfits, in a tangle of daily adventures that excludes neither heroism nor death, and still everyone stands to the real in the proportion of little figures seen in a stereoscope. This curious quality seems to me at once the flavor and the limitation of the novel. The wonder—the poetry—which in Dickens is released at every new human encounter, at every eccentricity and singularity of the crowd, finds in the autobiographical tone an imaginative coherence, especially in the pages on childhood, which welds every character, every caricature, into the field of the action. As long as childhood, and the recollection of it, lasts, the story of little David possesses a development, and he lives in a world constructed by the imagination. They are unforgettable pages, and each of us (I don't know greater praise) rediscovers in the narrative his own secret experience.

Having finished his studies, David enters upon life, and look how memory evaporates and is replaced by the technique of the actual event. The author's imagination is still that of the pages on childhood: sympathetic and entertained wonder in the face of human beings. These portraits are his whole poetry, but their movements no longer belong to a world composed in memory; they belong to an enormous and futile social reality where tragedies really happen. Hence the contrast and the effect of the stereoscope. But not even in the most absurd and declamatory pages (those which are dedicated to Martha) does Dickens lose the benefit of his refreshing candor. He has a sense of proportion, and his naiveté is more intellectual than technical. The "truth" of his world is also its charm. Above a background of unrealistic poetic justice there are born the surprising little figures like miniatures.

Here the well-known humor finds its roots. Dickens' "justice," founded on a fairy-tale morality, is too moralistic and too little poetical: it shows itself in his happiest moments in a smile, it lays bare no conscience. Even as the tone becomes agitated, the reader always awaits concrete explanations given with a smile, and the smile comes and settles the matter and takes it back to the sphere of plain common sense. Such justice is not poetic because it does not intimately configure a world where things happen that not only enchant or entertain as in childhood, but because of the light or responsibility with which they are invested ought to demand graver judgment. David, who has kept the point of view of childhood, plays with all seriousness at being a man, but I would be embarrassed to find in the chronicle of his life a point at which his initiation to manhood is concretized. You might even say that this is the novel of delayed development and of the hero's good intentions in making a man of himself—which his union with Agnes at the end of the book tells us, but does not show us, happened. Except that there are too many events in the book where life, while wishing to be reflected in its complexity, doesn't achieve a formal self-awareness of this complexity. Not even the humor, therefore, breaks the frame of the miniature: at most it colors it amiably. Justice, on so much human comedy, inconsistent and fairy-tale.

And yet it happens to us in reading this novel, as in reading the best novels of Balzac, to forget all critical sense, and to consent to the liveliness of the page, in the same way that we abandon ourselves to the adventurous fable of a film. The naive enthusiasm with which the narrators reconstruct their society is that in them which stimulates us. Still, we are far from the enormous and changeable Balzacian curiosity, from that taste for every mode, for every psychological and social type: Dickens is less red-blooded and less outspoken, but—at least in *David Copperfield*—he is equally, and perhaps more, transparent and genial. The fact is that his intention is more circumscribed: the unity of the panorama is not given by an external choice (scenes from the world of peasants or from the life of courtesans), but by the fundamental wonder of two good and ingenuous eyes which train themselves on people.

Differently from Balzac, who, the more he hammers a character, the more meaning he gets out of him, Dickens enchants our attention with the minor figures who flash an instant quite brightly and manage not to let themselves get caught in the external and moralistic mechanism of the events. How can we help thinking, at this point, of the various waiters with whom David makes bewildered acquaintance in his lodging houses? There is no shortage of these figures from the beginning of the book to the end. But I would say more: even the "great" characters are introduced in the same way, and they possess life in the degree that they flash all the time unexpectedly like caricatures. One thinks of Steerforth, the idol of David's life, the monster of extraordinary capacities and of abject vices, who, possessing for good and for ill everything that David lacks, passes through the novel forever desired and elusive. Dickens expresses his sense of wonder in this way. To the extent that not only the persons, but things, furniture, houses, cities, swarm, as in a Flemish canvas, detailed and surprising in their everyday clarity. So many are the roads that lead to poetry.

PREFACE TO JOSEPH CONRAD, *'TWIXT LAND AND SEA*

In the note prefixed to the first edition of this extraordinary triptych of tales the author insists that "notwithstanding their autobiographical form . . . [they] are not the record of personal experiences." Obviously. And the flavor of idle talk, of gossip gathered in the idleness of ports or sitting on the wicker chairs of tropical verandas, is entirely clear in the whole framework and the "asides" of these pages. They have been "heard," not "lived." It is after all a typical technique of Conrad's to play with speakers and to refract the facts through the mouths and sensibilities of many witnesses, to the degree that at a certain point you are bound to notice that the chief interest of the page resides less in the event than in the tone of the voice that relates it.

Still, as in all the good fiction of his generation, you feel that Conrad also, when he puts forth his best efforts, draws from a fund of memory and emotion which can be labeled with the title of one of his *novelle:* "Youth." There is no other way to explain the fact that when, as in the Napoleonic and South American or European stories, he abandons the oceanic circle of the horizon and, especially, of the Oriental seas which he sailed in the green years, he usually becomes long-winded or tired or distracted. While the regions of the Indian or of the Pacific Oceans, the lost islands, the human wreckage, the somnolent merchant marine shipping, the contrast between the gorgeous luminous nature and the quest for an obscurity, for a solitary oblivion—all that which was for him like the face of life itself glimpsed in the early years—never enters his page without a thrill, a tremor of sweetness and disquiet, a scent of a secret garden disclosed with a self-conscious and anxious hand. There is in Conrad an exoticism, a predilection for certain unusual and far-off places, which has nothing capricious about it. Of the many exotic writers of the end of the century (Loti, Kipling, London, Hudson) he is unquestionably the least "picturesque," the least given to rendering with a rich palette the touristic customs and colors which he happened to encounter. You might even say that he veils them, that he tends to deaden their full-flavored liveliness, and that he dissolves them all in an indistinct nostalgic and introspective haze which takes from them all materiality of things seen and washes them in as a monotonous but always magical present atmosphere. Here we are outside the picturesque choice, always hot in pursuit of superficial new angles of vision. Here the background has the obsession of an ordinary atmosphere, and so intense and inevitable is the presence of this "elsewhere," of this memory, that we actually seem to move in the enchanted circle of a symbol, of a myth. The South Seas are really for Conrad the place of the soul—not the high seas of

Melville, at once titanic and biblical, not that health resort of Stevenson's, rich with noble legends and interesting institutions, but the everlasting restless comings and goings of the coast, " 'twixt land and sea," the suspense that can make of every landing, of every well-known, banal, predictable landing, the beginning of a magnificent and absurd adventure of youth, of passion, and of destiny.

Here it begins to be clear that the exotic country fuses in Conrad with the ardor of the soul which in its evenings witnesses the disenchanted reswarming of the adolescent dreams. It *is* this ardor; and the quiet intensity of the familiar memory incarnates it for us as a symbol. And as the exotic country is constantly implied in the narrative, filtered and refracted through a subtle play of familiar atmospheres, so the ardent, romantic, naive world of mystery and adventure—the imprisoned lady, the fugitive rebel, the two perfect lovers of this book—passes from mouth to mouth, refracts itself in ordinary psychologies, becomes wisdom and comment, and turns back upon itself, made ironic, saddened, disguised. Each of these tales is like the dream of an adolescent who, afraid of himself and of the great world, hides himself and saves himself behind the banal conventions of conversation and daily life. From no other root are born the protagonists, the "I's," and the Jacobuses, the Nelson-Nielsons who populate this book and with changed names the whole tropical forest of Conrad's "Malaysian" novels. The taste for idle chatter, for introducing and developing the event as in the amiable and rambling eloquence of the experienced old man of many memories, who especially likes to linger over the most singular and the most eccentric types whom he has known, and which makes not for impressionism but because of the grand passion, of the absurd dream that couldn't be realized, he doesn't dare to declare himself a participant and among maxims, sentences, and self-ironies bitterly plays around his theme—this taste, the unmistakable Conrad touch, ends by definitively imposing itself as the true drama, the true theme of his narrative. For it is in this merciless and disconsolate play that these three *novelle,* like the greater novels—*Lord Jim* and *Victory*—touch the heights of poetry. Of a book by Conrad you remember in general neither the character nor the action—these are muffled in the interplay of the levels, of the allusions, and of the testimonies—you remember the tortuous, tenacious, desperately faithful and sorrowful passion to recall, to linger over a dear and distant horizon while a dream, an anguish, a remorse, constrains the heart, to chatter perhaps about something indifferent.

Here is born Conrad's irresistible human appeal, his manly and modest piety, which sympathizes with and reduces every more tragic and foolish experience to a key of stoic resignation. Someone in this compassion has wanted to see an ethnic sign of Conrad's Slavic origins. But this racist method of isolating the individual from the society and culture in which he lives seems to me to have had its day. The pietism of a Tolstoy or of a Dostoevsky originates in ethical and religious preoccupations from which Conrad is alien—it is not for nothing that his favorite Russians were Turgenev and Chekhov, and after all he admired Maupassant and Flaubert much more. Neither is his compassion an almost voluptuous abandonment to humiliation and suffering, a mystical need for expiation. Having grown up in Anglo-Saxon surroundings, Conrad maintains before the enigma, before the anguish of living, an ironic and resigned dignity; he shrugs his shoulders, and with clenched teeth, even if unconvinced, he stands at the breach and lends a hand, always detached, always correct, always the gentleman. That alter ego who, at the end of the second *novella,* "had lowered himself into the water to take his punishment: a free man, a proud swimmer striking out for a new destiny," emerges from a lineage of heroes, not of saints.

ROBERT LOUIS STEVENSON

The centenary of the birth of Robert L. Stevenson, which will fall on November 13th of this year, probably won't much change the ambiguous reputation which the author of *Treasure Island* enjoys. Criticism has not yet emerged from the difficulty of reconciling admiration for the brightness and fairy-tale liveliness of his page—that quality which makes R. L. S. dear to and accepted even by juvenile readers—with the lack of so-called profundity, of problematical seriousness, of every apparent social and human interest. It is not an accident, they say, that R. L. S. should have written a book entitled *The New Arabian Nights:* the characters of his romances, of his tales, of his fables, always have the air of moving in a rarefied, picturesque atmosphere of mere one-dimensional fantasy, exactly as happens, or seems to happen, with the Arabian storyteller. And indeed, they remember, R. L. S., who was always ill, preoccupying himself exclusively with problems of style and fine invention, ended his life in the hermitage of Samoa, far from the tumult and from the problems of his country and society.

At this point we might remember that the case of R. L. S. was not isolated and that practically all Western culture of his time (the end of the nineteenth and the beginning of the twentieth century) went through this crisis of disgust for the environment and, in one way or another, even when it didn't physically travel to the end of the world, sought for itself a paradise and a justification. It was a way, like another, of arguing, that is to say, of living, with your own culture. But I should simply like—overlooking that which R. L. S. didn't dream of giving us—to discover and utilize so much (little or great) as he has given us, in other words, to estimate the importance of it and the trace left on European culture of the new century.

The narrative mode that R. L. S. found operative in his country and abroad when, around 1880, he commenced to flourish, was mainly concerned with the problems and difficulties of realism, otherwise called naturalism—that is to say, it was concerned with the task of objectively describing and recreating society in its most neglected and quotidian and brutal aspects. Strange as it may seem, this realism was only one aspect of incipient aestheticism, the tendency, that is, to seek in art, and in life, the powerful sensation, the sensation rare and vital, in which to solace yourself and isolate yourself. The inheritance of the Olympian artists who flourished about mid-century—Stendhal, Balzac, Thackeray, Dickens, the great Russians—was stirring and springing to life now in the explorations and discoveries which today bear the names of Thomas Hardy and Oscar Wilde, Flaubert, Maupassant and Zola, Verga and D'Annunzio. Well, Stevenson's really singular position seems to me this: he was neither a realist nor an aesthete—or, if you prefer, he was both these things, and he was such without intending it, without proposing it to himself, and he went directly, instinctively, to whatever was ultimately living, genuine, eternal in the demands of the two schools.

Certainly, his most immediate masters were Flaubert and Maupassant and Mérimée. Which means that with R. L. S. there enters English prose narrative, assuming there an exotic fascination, the lesson of style of the French naturalists, the choice of the exact word, irreplaceable, the sense of color, of sound, of the essential nuance, of the precisely observed detail —and at the same time the aversion to any romantic or sentimental excess, the taste for an almost stoic sobriety and self-control. This, in my opinion, and in passing, remains the most authentic and operative fruit of realistic aestheticism, and this discipline of a clear, craftsmanlike, sober, and "functional" kind of writing seems to me worth much more than the long-winded, pseudoscientific investigations of a Zola or the mystical-heroic intoxications of D'Annunzio and company. In this sense, that he was a craftsmanlike devotee of the word and of the passage, R. L. S. is indebted to the French. But he was also a fabulist, to whom any journalistic and gossiping complacency in bourgeois "objectivity" is finally alien, one who retains the precision and the truth of the sentence, of the sensation, of the gesture, in order to render palpable and familiar the nostalgias, the braveries, the loyalties, and the heroisms of the eternal adventures of the boy who enters the world. To dissociate the "realistic" style of his age from the program of pseudoscientific social investigation which was congenital with it, as well as from the decadent taste for the sensation as an end in itself, and to apply it instead to storytelling, breathless storytelling, this was a gesture unconsciously revolutionary and rich for the future.

You might say that the most valid writing of our century commences here (though not only here, of course)—on the one hand the refusal to search for poetry in the brutally human document, and on the other the condemnation of any aestheticism which tries to avoid facts. Americans, Russians, English, French, and Italians, all owe something to this example of a craft exercised with the stoic naiveté of a boy who believes naturally in life and in the imagination.

INDEX
OF NAMES